Sociology

Sociology

An Introduction

Ken Roberts

University of Liverpool, UK

Edward Elgar
Cheltenham, UK • Northampton, MA, USA

Published by
Edward Elgar Publishing Limited
The Lypiatts
15 Lansdown Road
Cheltenham
Glos GL50 2JA
UK

Edward Elgar Publishing, Inc.
William Pratt House
9 Dewey Court
Northampton
Massachusetts 01060
USA

A catalogue record for this book
is available from the British Library

Library of Congress Control Number: 2011932899

MIX
Paper from
responsible sources
FSC
www.fsc.org
FSC® C018575

ISBN 978 0 85793 019 4 (cased)
      978 0 85793 021 7 (paperback)

Typeset by Servis Filmsetting Ltd, Stockport, Cheshire
Printed and bound by MPG Books Group, UK

Contents

List of tables

1. Introduction

WHAT IS SOCIOLOGY?

Sociology is an accessible subject; more so than most academic disciplines. Students can start from scratch at any stage – lower or upper secondary, undergraduate or postgraduate. It is even possible to switch into sociology later on without any formal sociology qualifications. There are no rigid entry requirements at any level. Late entrants compensate, often more than compensate, with their knowledge of other subjects (economics, politics, media studies, history, geography and many others), or with experience in employment on shop floors or in management, or broader social experience in grass roots politics, trade unions, charities, as parents or youth leaders. A danger lies in the impression that anyone can do sociology and that you need only common sense. However, there is a difference between just 'doing' and 'doing well'.

One of the attractions of sociology for students, teachers and researchers is the wide range of topics that is offered. Sociology has something that will surely interest everyone – crime, sex, the family, alcohol, migration, football, race relations and many more. It appears that any topic can be accommodated in sociology, and this appearance is not deceptive. Sociology can offer a spokesperson to the media on virtually any news item. The syllabuses for sociology programmes have the appearance of menus from which students can pick and mix according to their interests. It is possible to treat sociology as a series of social studies, but not without missing most of what sociology can uniquely offer.

If sociology was just a bundle of social studies it would be losing a long-term battle for survival as its topics developed their own experts and became independent disciplines – economics and politics, then criminology, social policy, education, family studies, urban studies, sexology, leisure studies and so on. Sociology would now be suffering the fate of philosophy – once the whole of knowledge but now left with 'What is it possible to know?' with the natural sciences, then the arts, humanities and social sciences all having departed. Sociology is different because there is a distinctive sociological approach to the economy, politics and everything else. A problem has always been the difficulty in offering a concise statement of what makes sociology distinctive. This book is such an attempt: a few sentences will not suffice. The problem is that all concise definitions of sociology are portals to perpetual debates within the discipline.

Sociology is the study of society or societies. All sociologists can recite and will agree with this statement. This is a literal meaning of the word 'sociology'. We study whole societies (hence sociology encompasses all social issues), but a society might mean world society, a country, or a smaller unit such as a sports club. Sociology can operate at any of these levels. In practice, sociology's societies have usually been countries, but sociologists will agree that the country, the state, is just one of several levels of social life on which they can focus. Some claim that current globalising trends are making countries less independent, more interdependent, and that the sociological gaze must shift upwards. It may simultaneously need to shift downwards in order to grasp some implications of globalisation such as international trade moving industries from older to newer industrial countries, and thereby stripping some localities of employment.

There are further problems in defining 'society' and the 'social'. What are the basic elements, the 'matter', from which societies and the social are constituted? Here sociologists resort to analogies. Some define their subject matter as social facts, regular and recurrent patterns of behaviour represented by crime rates, fertility rates, unemployment rates and so on. These facts are said to be linked together to form a social structure, analogous to a building, or a social system, analogous to a machine with connected parts. Other sociologists say that their basic subject matter is more analogous to a conversation, and that the elements of social life are the symbols (like language), discourses and meanings with which people form social relationships with one another.

Sociologists will agree that sociology is a social science, but they can agree only because this term can have different meanings. It can mean that sociology is a social *science*; different from other kinds of enquiry, and producing a different kind of knowledge, because its methods are basically the same as those of the natural sciences. Alternatively, sociology can be defined as a *social* science, whose methods and knowledge must be different from those of the natural sciences because humans are different from inanimate matter.

Sociology is a subject within which students and teachers debate endlessly 'What is society?' and 'In what sense can the study of society be scientific?' These are serious issues with which everyone in sociology has to engage, but most students do not enter, and most teachers and researchers do not remain in sociology solely for this kind of intellectual stimulation.

Rather, we all need to adopt at least tentative and temporary positions on these issues in order to address the topics in which we are really interested. As we have seen, there are many such topics, but if we ask what is distinctive about how these topics are approached in sociology, we find two sets of distinctively sociological concerns.

TRANSFORMATIONS AND DIVISIONS

First, the whole of sociology has always been, and still is, about major historical changes, here called transformations. Such changes can have occurred at any time and in any place, but in practice sociologists have always focused on the transformations that have produced their own societies. Sociology was born in the nineteenth century, in Europe. That was where and when the word 'sociology' was first used. With the advantage of historical distance, we can now view the nineteenth century as the period when European countries were experiencing a particular stage in their longer-term modernisation, a process that began in the seventeenth and eighteenth centuries, during the Age of Reason when instead of following traditions and accepting religious authority, people began addressing questions on the basis of reason and evidence. An outcome was the birth of modern science, which was associated with rapid improvements in technology which permitted the exploration of the world, the expansion of trade and the development of modern empires, and in Europe during the nineteenth century the outcomes were industrialisation, urbanisation and demands for democracy. Today we can understand these changes only because we now have these words, which were given their present-day meanings during the birth of sociology. Some argue that the modern era is now closing and that we are entering post-modern times. By the twenty-second century this view might have been proved correct. Meantime, in most of the world, modernisation is an ongoing process. Countries that digressed into Fascism and Communism have rejoined the global mainstream. Late-developing, new industrialising countries are just beginning to experience modernisation. The nineteenth-century founders of sociology are still on all syllabuses because the trends that they identified and tried to explain are still ongoing, their explanations are still alive, and still contested.

In Europe during the nineteenth century, industrialisation and urbanisation transformed the lives of most people in the relevant countries. Since then the most advanced modern societies have experienced further transformations, which have always set new agendas for sociology. One such transformation followed the Second World War when West European and North American countries became 'social democracies'. They developed 'social market economies', where the economies were managed to serve wider social objectives rather than the rest of the societies adapting to the economies (as had been the case during industrialisation). Among other things, the economies generated the wealth to support welfare states which offered 'security' – adequate incomes, health care according to need, the full range of educational opportunities and decent housing – to all citizens. Today the relevant countries retain legacies from this era just as Soviet Communism incorporated legacies from Tsarist rule, and today's post-Communist countries carry legacies from Communism. Since the Second World War and up to the present day, sociology has assessed the achievements and limitations of social democracy.

During the closing decades of the twentieth century Western countries experienced a further transformation. Their economies became post-industrial, absorbed new information and communication technologies (ICT), and intercountry flows of information, capital, goods, services and people (the trends described as globalisation) increased in volume. The new economies have been described as knowledge economies. The new era has been labelled an information age. We shall need greater historical distance before we can finally decide which label or labels are the most appropriate. Amid these changes, the new tendency has been to cap or roll back state welfare. Governments have abandoned the social market in favour of neo-liberal economic policies which once more force the rest of the societies to adapt to economic requirements rather than vice versa. New industrial countries have leapt straight into the advanced modern age. They have been able to industrialise using the very latest technologies, 'unencumbered' by the kinds of state welfare still carried by the older industrial countries.

Sociologists usually specialise on topics in which they have a special interest, and in which they develop special expertise, but what makes them all sociologists is their common interest in how what is happening in education, football, the family or whatever is situated in a particular era, a product and part of an ongoing or past transformation.

The second distinctive feature which makes work sociological is its attention to social divisions. Again, this has been the case since the birth of sociology. We recognise that transformations are unlikely to affect all sections of a population in the same way or to the same extent. The outcomes are likely to depend on social class (positions in the systems of economic production and distribution) and gender. They may also differ between ethnic groups, according to age, possibly sexual orientation, and whether people suffer from disabilities. Also, historical changes do not just happen. They are instigated, or at least shaped by humans, most likely from a particular section of a population defined by class, gender and so on, and with sectional interests.

This does not mean that a particular division, or a group thus defined, is a main focus in all sociological enquiries, though this is often the case. It does mean that whatever they are investigating sociologists can be relied on to explore the significance of class and gender, and possibly other divisions, depending on the topic and the society in question.

Students can be drawn to sociology, and teachers and researchers may stay in the subject on account of the opportunity to concentrate on issues in which they are especially interested, but if done properly, sociology offers far more. Sociology can tell us all who we are by helping us to locate ourselves within our societies, usually via our families and class positions, gender and ethnic groups, and geography. Sociology can finesse the placements by adding other divisions – sexual orientation and so on. Sociology tells us what it means in terms of life chances (what we can make of our lives) to occupy a particular social location. From sociology we can also learn about the character of the countries in which we live, where we are probably, but not necessarily, citizens, and the country's place in world history and in the world today. Sociology will deliver all this if done properly, never losing sight of social divisions, or how the present is a product of past and ongoing social transformations.

THE BOOK

This is not a textbook that tries to tell students all that will be required in an introductory course. It is a guide to what is inside, if sociology is done properly. So Chapters 2 and 3 are about what sociology has to say about the three transformations (the last of which is still far from complete) that have produced the oldest, and in this sense the most advanced, modern societies in Europe and North America – the countries that experienced industrialisation, became social democracies (albeit in somewhat different ways and to different extents in different countries), and have now entered a post-industrial age. Chapters 4 and 5 are about the main social divisions that feature throughout sociology (by social class, gender and ethnicity), and other divisions (by age, sexual orientation and disability) that are now claiming space on sociology's agenda. These chapters review how all these divisions have been reshaped, and have become more or less prominent, as a result of successive large-scale social transformations.

Chapters 6 and 7 are about the perpetual, apparently unresolvable, issues that sociologists debate. What is society? What is special about the knowledge produced by sociology's methods? Can this knowledge be described as objective? In what sense if any can this knowledge be labelled scientific? Fortunately, different views on these matters do not prevent all parties adding to our knowledge and understanding of social transformations and divisions.

Chapter 8 considers the social role of sociology. The subject offers understanding, but throughout its history the attractions have included the possibility of learning enough to make a difference. Sociologists, given their discipline, realise that their impact will be governed by the character of the societies in which they work, and their places within the societies' social divisions. We know that nowadays we can be 'professional' sociologists, speaking mainly to one another. We can also be 'policy sociologists', conducting research and developing knowledge at the behest of government departments and other organsiations. We know that this role is likely to turn us into servants of power. We can be 'critical sociologists' a variant of professional sociology, offering (mainly to one another) searing critiques of the unjust world in which we live and work. We may wear different 'hats' on different occasions and at different career stages. Another possible role is developing a 'public sociology', partnered by users in social movements which mobilise for change. This is probably the most appealing and simultaneously the most difficult role available to sociology.

Of course, as well as describing, this book is advocating sociology. When the subject was created there were no specialist social sciences such as economics, political science, urban studies and all the other specialisms. These are all later arrivals. Sociology is not a 'gap filler' but remains, as always, the general social science. Its contention is that the fragmentation of knowledge into separate social sciences prevents us understanding anything. Sociology is ambitious. It is a challenging subject. The project seeks to encompass all parts of all societies throughout the present-day world and throughout history. This project is incomplete. No one person can be expected to know everything. Sociology is a collective enterprise. The project is still worthwhile and needs students who will keep the ambition alive.

2. Transformations: modernisation and industrialisation

INTRODUCTION

Social transformations are particular kinds of social change. Change has occurred whenever a society at time B differs from its state at time A. Transformations are especially thorough changes. When such change is complete, which is most likely to take decades or even centuries rather than years, people will feel that they inhabit or are entering a wholly new era. Such changes may begin in politics where there is a change of system rather than just a routine change in rulers. When such change leads to a social transformation we say that a revolution has occurred, as with the French Revolution (1789–1799). When there is a non-routine change of government but no wider transformation, all that has happened is regime change.

Sociology was born during the industrial transformation of European countries (the changes that are called the Industrial Revolution in Britain). Sociology's agenda at that time was identifying the sources of the changes that were underway, charting the character of the new era, and investigating its problems. Western sociologists have always devoted most of their attention to changes in their own countries. As explained in Chapter 1, the agenda shifted after the Second World War when another transformation was underway, this time associated with the rise to power of social-democratic political parties, the maintenance of full employment, steady economic growth at an unprecedented rate, the spread of prosperity, and the creation of welfare states which made education, health care and income maintenance for vulnerable groups, and for everyone at vulnerable points in the life course, into rights of citizenship. Housing, transport and leisure services were partly incorporated into these welfare agendas. The most recent transformation that occupies today's sociologists is into the post-industrial, some say a second modern or even post-modern age.

There have been many other transformations during world history – the rise and decline of the ancient civilisations of the Middle East and Mediterranean; the rebirth of Europe after the Dark Age that followed the collapse of the Roman Empire; the rise and decline of modern European Empires, including the British Empire; the rise and decline of Fascism and Communism in twentieth-century Europe; and the more recent birth of new industrial societies in Asia and Latin America. These transformations are treated as specialist topics in Western sociology whose core agenda has been set by the three transformations in Western countries themselves. All agree that the rise of industrial society was a genuine transformation, the great transformation of modern times. It was not the start of the process, but industrialisation was the big step propelling the population masses into the modern age. British historians refer to the nineteenth century as the great historical divide: at the beginning roughly 80 per cent of the population lived in rural areas whereas at the end around 80 per cent were living in industrial towns and cities. There are disputes as to whether the changes that followed the Second World War, and those associated with the decline of employment in manufacturing, the advent of the latest information and communication technologies (ICT), and late-twentieth-century globalisation amount to genuine transformations. Thus sociology's agenda has been about transformations that are agreed, alleged and sometimes disputed.

THE BIRTH OF SOCIOLOGY

Sociology was founded in the nineteenth century in the sense that the term was coined then by a Frenchman, Auguste Comte (1798–1857). His kind of thinking was not wholly new, but Comte wished to distinguish his ideas from all that had gone before. His sociology was to be a science. This was the era when the natural sciences were beginning to enjoy huge prestige. Their achievements were evident in progress in transport and manufacturing. The Enlightenment, alternatively known as the Age of Reason, an intellectual movement that spread from the late-seventeenth century and continued throughout the eighteenth century, had freed social thought from religious authority and dogma. The complementary and necessary step, in Comte's view, was to base theories on evidence.

Comte believed that history was driven by the development of human thought, a view he shared with his German contemporary, Georg Hegel (see below). Comte believed that history had developed through three stages (his law of three stages). First, in a theological stage, events were explained as the work of a wind spirit, a fire spirit and so on. Subsequently, in a metaphysical stage, events were explained in terms of abstract forces such as natural law or the will of God. Finally, in the scientific stage, explanations were in terms of laws of cause and effect, based on observations, experiments and comparisons. Comte believed that the scientific study of society would lead to equivalent progress to that achieved by the natural sciences. This is why he labelled his sociology 'positivist'. Subsequently this term came to mean attempts to mirror the methods of the natural sciences, but Comte's intention was to associate sociology with improvement against those who deplored the end of the old ways of life, the passing of traditional society and the demise of old aristocratic regimes (see Andreski, 1974; Thompson, 1976).

Although in the vanguard of industrialisation, Britain was not a principal birthplace of sociological thought. The Scottish moral philosophers included Adam Smith (1723–1790), author of *The Wealth of Nations*, first published in 1776, who identified the benign invisible hand of the market. Britain was also the home of the principal utilitarian philosophers (Jeremy Bentham and John Stuart Mill) who advocated 'the greatest happiness for the greatest number'. The ideas of these thinkers were to be absorbed into economics and political science, when these disciplines were formed. Until the late-nineteenth century all the above were contributing to political economy or political philosophy. At that time no one was employed as a sociologist or economist.

Comte's law of three stages was about the differences between the emergent and earlier historical eras, and the forces that were driving change. Thus sociology was conceived as the study of social structure and change (the terms that would subsequently be used). This became sociology's agenda. The actual ideas of Comte soon died; likewise the ideas of many other nineteenth-century social theorists. The names of those theorists whose ideas live on, who are now regarded as founding fathers of sociology, the source of the original sociological theories, are: Karl Marx, Émile Durkheim and Max Weber, sometimes known as sociology's holy trinity.

We need to be clear that it is only retrospectively that these particular figures have been recognised as founders of sociology. Comte believed that he was founding a new discipline. So did Durkheim, who established Europe's first university department of sociology at Bourdeaux (France) in 1895. Karl Marx did not regard himself a sociologist. He spent his life trying to create a revolutionary political movement, not an academic discipline. Max Weber never held a post as a sociologist. He was recognised as such by contemporaries in Germany who held posts in sociology, but history, law and economics also have claims to Weber's legacy.

Comte, Marx, Durkheim and Weber were certainly not the only nineteenth- and early-twentieth-century figures who offered explanations of the course of history within which ongoing changes could be set. Their names live on, in Comte's case because he invented the term 'sociology', but otherwise because their ideas have not died. Present-day sociology students are unlikely to hear much, if anything, about Arthur de Gobineau (1816–1882), one of the original sources of racial theories, Herbert Spencer (1820–1903), Leonard T. Hobhouse (1864–1929) who was Britain's first Professor of Sociology (at the London School of Economics from 1907), or the Italian Vilfredo Pareto (1848–1923). Until the Second World War all these names would have featured prominently in an introduction to sociology. Herbert Spencer, the British polymath, an expert on virtually everything and world-famous during his lifetime, anticipated many of Durkheim's ideas; but it is Durkheim, whose sociological contributions were far more substantial, who has become recognised as a founding father.

Sociology had somewhat different origins in North America, basically because America had no feudal past, no aristocracy and an associated socio-political order to overthrow. American sociology developed from the 1890s, centred at the University of Chicago until the Second World War. It was inspired primarily by the transformation of America from a land of rural communities into a mainly urban civilisation. Some European sociologists, most notably the German Ferdinand Tönnies, made the rural-urban contrast the centre piece of their contrasts between the old and the new. However, most of the Europe's nineteenth- and early-twentieth-century social theorists treated urbanisation as an outcome of the underlying forces that were driving change: the development of human thought according to Comte; as we shall see the development of capitalism according to Marx; the division of labour according to Durkheim; and rationalisation according to Weber.

Later chapters in this book explain that, from its birth, American sociology was based on research into current social (mainly urban) conditions. After the Second World War sociology spread rapidly and widely across higher education in both Europe and North America, drawing together Europe's social theories and the kind of fact gathering, the social statistics that Comte had wanted to distinguish from his sociology.

KARL MARX (1818–1883) AND CAPITALISM

Marx was born and educated in Germany, became a revolutionary while still a student, and lived in London from 1849 onwards. At that time Britain was more tolerant of residents with revolutionary ideas, even foreign-born residents, than other European capitals. By 1849 Marx was already collaborating with Friedrich Engels (1820–1895), another young German revolutionary. Engels was from a German textile manufacturing family. Marx's father was a lawyer. Both of Marx's parents were born Jewish but had converted to Lutheranism. In 1843 Marx married a daughter of a Prussian baron. Both Marx and Engels were from thoroughly bourgeois backgrounds. Engels' family business took him to Manchester, where he wrote a book on the condition of the English working class based on his experience in Manchester and Salford. This book brought Engels to the attention of Marx and they became collaborators until Marx's death in 1883 (Engels lived until 1895).

Marx did not regard himself as an academic, armchair scientist. He believed that he was producing the ideas that would inspire and become the basis of a revolutionary European-wide political movement. He is the only nineteenth-century thinker, now claimed by sociology as a founding father, whose name not only became an *ism* but also one of the twentieth century's most successful change ideologies. A debate on whether Marx was really a sociologist raged until the 1950s when the verdict became 'yes'. Previously Marxism had been more likely to feature among the topics studied by sociology – as an ideology and movement – rather than an integral part of the discipline itself. However, by the 1970s Marxism had become one of the most influential theories in Western sociology. Since then it has been securely housed, though it is also claimed by politics, philosophy and many other academic disciplines: sociology does not have exclusive property rights.

Georg Hegel (1770–1831) remained a towering intellectual colossus in Germany throughout Marx's lifetime. Hegel addressed philosophy's core problem: what can be known to be true? Like Comte, Hegel believed that history was driven by the development of human thought. Unlike Comte, Hegel did not believe that thought had progressed through just three stages. Hegel argued that thought and knowledge developed through a continuous dialectical process in which accepted truths were contested, which led to new ideas, which were then contested and that this process was ongoing. Thesis bred antithesis which led to a synthesis which became the new thesis and so on. Hegel believed that this cycle would end only when thought had arrived at absolute truth which was beyond challenge. He managed to convince himself that this point was close to arriving in the Prussia of his day, a view that endeared him to the authorities (see Singer, 1983).

Marx was among the young Hegelians who disagreed profoundly. Even before completing his studies in Berlin, Marx was arguing that the human condition in the society of his time was characterised by alienation, meaning that people were separated from their true selves, unable to exercise genuine control over their lives. In Marx's view, history would need to turn at least another full cycle before humanity fulfilled its potential. If Hegel was an idealist (history driven by ideas) Marx was a materialist.

He believed that work, not thought, was the most basic human activity. People needed to work on nature in order to survive. He also believed that ideas arose within, and tended to reflect concerns and interests derived from material conditions. Fulfilling their potential depended above all else on people having control over their own labour power.

In 1848 Marx and Engels, then aged 30 and 28, co-authored their famous political tract, the *Communist Manifesto* (Marx and Engels, 1848). This was a call to arms: 1848 was a year of attempted revolutions in a series of European capitals. The original aims of the French Revolution – liberty, fraternity, equality – had been perverted. Until the First World War most of Europe continued to be ruled by monarchs and aristocratic regimes: the Austro-Hungarian Empire, the Ottoman Empire (then in decline), the Russian Empire and the German states which were unified in 1871. Throughout the nineteenth century 'the mob' was a political force that all European rulers feared. In 1789 the Paris mob had begun to guillotine the country's royals and aristocrats.

From 1849 Marx lived in London, often close to poverty, supported by his main patron, Engels, spasmodic earnings from journalism and allowances from his wife's family. His main work was the writing of *Capital*, an analysis of the capitalist system that was becoming economically ascendant throughout Europe. The book explained how capitalism worked, and why its own dynamics would lead to its ultimate destruction.

The basic claims of Marxism were, and still are:

- In order to subsist people need to cooperate, to enter into social relationships with one another (relationships of production).
- Collaboratively people develop the forces of production (natural resources and the tools to work on these resources).
- Once people can produce a surplus (more than required to meet their bare subsistence needs and to allow the population to reproduce) as a result of developing the forces of production, it is possible for there to be a division between workers (producers) and a class of owners who, together with priests, state officials, artists and other non-producers, appropriate the surplus.
- The relationships of production that prevail at any time will be those that are best able to exploit the current forces of production, and within the prevailing relationships the forces of production will be developed to the maximum possible extent.
- However, points are reached when the forces of production cannot be fully exploited within the prevailing relationships of production.
- This creates a potentially revolutionary situation. The time is then ripe for a subordinate class, or a faction thereof, to seize control of

the forces of production, reset the relationships of production, then fully exploit and further develop the forces of production.

Marx and Engels believed that this was how societies had progressed from an original state of primitive Communism, through the ancient civilisations, then through feudalism, on to capitalism, which in turn would give way to socialism. They believed that the capitalist system that was spreading across Europe was dividing the populations into two main classes. There was the bourgeoisie, the capitalist class, the owners of factories, mines, railways, shipping lines and so on. Juxtaposed to the owners was the proletariat, the workers, who sold their labour power to employers who appropriated surplus value. Each class needed and could not exist without the other. Other classes that could be identified in nineteenth-century Europe – mainly self-employed craft workers and merchants, independent professionals and peasants – were expected to be absorbed into one of the two great classes of the new age.

Marx and Engels were impressed by the productive power of capitalism. They believed that the forces of production that this system was developing would enable all people to live free from hardship. Yet they also believed that capitalist relationships of production condemned the proletariat to lives that fluctuated around the subsistence level. This was a glaring contradiction. Once perceived by the workers, aided by the theories that intellectuals such as Marx would supply, the proletariat was expected to mature from 'a class in itself' into a 'class for itself', to seize control of the forces of production and usher in an age of freedom and plenty. Everyone's material needs would be met. Simultaneously, people would escape from alienation: collectively they would control the forces of production and be in control of their lives. 'Bread' and 'freedom' are the twin promises that have mobilised millions behind the red flag.

Marx died without his hopes of becoming the leader of a successful socialist movement being fulfilled. On most matters of detail subsequent history has proved Marx wrong. He believed that conditions were growing ripe for revolution in his own lifetime, and that revolution was most likely in the most advanced capitalist country, which was Britain at that time. In the event, there has never been a proletarian revolution and a Communist government installed in any advanced capitalist country. In the twenty-first century, capitalism looks more firmly entrenched, and is an even more global system, than ever before. However, it is still possible to argue that capitalism's contradictions will ultimately result in its downfall. The bourgeoisie may have retained the upper hand in the class struggle up to now, but it remains possible to insist that this struggle, this dialectic, a materialist dialectic, continues to drive history forward. Owners continue to devise new ways of enlarging their wealth and extracting surplus value. Simultaneously, workers try to gain larger shares of the wealth that their labour creates, and greater control of their lives in their workplaces and beyond. Marxists do not accept that that there has yet been another equivalent societal transformation since the rise of capitalism, and claim that their analysis has always correctly identified the fundamentals of the capitalist era (see McClellan, 1975; Reiss, 1996).

Marx may not have lived to see his ideas triumph in any country, but by the time of his death in 1883 his ideas were impossible to ignore. By the end of the nineteenth and throughout the greater part of the twentieth century there were political movements bearing his name throughout Europe. After the 1917 Bolshevik Revolution in Russia and up to the present day there have been governments that describe themselves as Marxist. Moreover, it is possible to regard the entire non-Marxist social sciences (political science and economics as well as sociology) as attempts to formulate alternative accounts of how European and North American societies have changed since the eighteenth century.

ÉMILE DURKHEIM (1858–1917) AND THE DIVISION OF LABOUR

Durkheim became Europe's first professional sociologist when he founded a sociology department at the University of Bordeaux in 1895. During the next 50 years sociology would spread slowly in the continent's universities. Departments with sociology in their titles were founded in England at the London School of Economics and the University of Manchester between 1903 and 1905.

If we discount Comte whose ideas are no longer alive, Durkheim is the sole founding father of sociology who saw himself unambiguously in such terms. Marx and Max Weber (see below), were both subsequently adopted by sociology. Like Marx, Durkheim was of Jewish descent and also like Marx he lived an entirely secular life. The biographies of these founding fathers are sometimes cited as evidence of the advantages that a marginal social position offers in cultivating a sociological imagination: it is necessary to examine one's own society as if from the outside or from the margins rather than as a fully immersed and committed participant. Durkheim paid little if any attention to Marx, who was then viewed as a political figure rather than a figure of scientific importance. Durkheim recognised his fellow Frenchman, Auguste Comte, as an intellectual predecessor. Durkheim's objections were not to Comte's aims. He shared Comte's ambition to create a science of society. Durkheim's objection was that Comte had not been truly scientific. Durkheim's own work was wide-ranging. He laid out 'rules' of sociological method that we will consider in Chapter 7. However, his earliest work was on the division of labour where he outlined his lifelong views on how and why the European societies of his day were changing (Durkheim, 1893).

Whereas Comte and Marx both saw history as a series of distinct stages, Durkheim believed that change had occurred more smoothly, incrementally. The master trend for Durkheim was the progressive division of labour. He speculated that the initial spark might have been increased population density, but believed that once in motion the trend became self-perpetuating. Earlier societies were said to have been simpler societies. At that time Europe's knowledge about earlier, 'primitive' societies was based on the reports of social anthropologists who had followed the spread of empires and documented the natives' customs, beliefs and ways of life. These were believed to be simpler versions of the most advanced societies. Thus Durkheim selected the Australian aborigines in order to identify the most elementary form of religious life (Durkheim, 1912). Asian societies, like the pre-modern civilisations of the Middle East and Mediterranean, were believed to be positioned somewhere between the primitive and the most advanced. Max Weber (see below) was to be an exception, but until Durkheim's lifetime all social theorists appear to have believed that all societies were following (or stalled at an early or intermediate stage) along the same evolutionary course.

For Durkheim, 'order' was the fundamental sociological problem. What made orderly social life possible? How did societies cohere? Thomas Hobbes (1588–1679), a seventeenth-century English political philosopher, had argued that the only alternative to a state of nature in which life was nasty, brutish and short was for everyone to submit to an all-powerful Leviathan, a monarch. Subsequently philosophers such as John Locke (1632–1704), another Englishman, and Jean-Jacques Rousseau (1712–1788), a Frenchman, argued that humans possessed natural rights and would only submit to a government under an implicit social contract within which their rights were protected. Marx's answer to the problem of order was that a dominant class oppressed the exploited using a combination of law, ideology and brute force when necessary. Durkheim had an entirely different answer.

Durkheim identified two solidifying processes whose relative importance changed as a society evolved from the simple to the complex. He believed that simple societies, where all members led similar lives and where there was little role differentiation, were bound by mechanical solidarity. There was a strong *conscience collective* (*conscience* simultaneously conveying the meanings of the English words conscience and

consciousness). People shared similar beliefs. There were rules that everyone was expected to obey. If and when rules were broken the *conscience
collective* would be outraged. The people would demand retribution –
punishment proportionate to the offence, maybe an eye for an eye. The
purpose of punishment was not to reform or rehabilitate the offender,
or somehow to rectify the wrong, but rather to quench the people's outraged feelings. Punishment enabled a community to re-assert its beliefs,
and all but the offender could confirm that they were on the side of right.
Durkheim believed that some deviance, rule-breaking, was inevitable and
indeed useful. A society where the *conscience collective* was so powerful as
to maintain total conformity would be oppressive and there would be no
innovation. This apart, it was necessary to have offenders in order for a
society to periodically celebrate its values, to demonstrate which kinds of
behaviour would not be tolerated, and to remind everyone of the relative
gravity of different offences. Deterrence was another useful outcome of
punishment.

Durkheim was a Professor of Education as well as of Sociology, and
he held distinctive views on the importance of schooling. He believed that
the school and the classroom were where the child learnt to submit to the
will of a group that was larger than the family. There had to be rules in
schools, and offenders had to be punished, but the punishment never had
to be so severe as to attract sympathy to the offender. Atypically for his
time, Durkheim was opposed to any physical punishments in schools.

As societies became more complex with specialist institutions for education, health care, welfare, different kinds of manufacturing, and hundreds
of specialised occupations, the *conscience collective* inevitably weakened,
though without becoming extinct. As this happened, Durkheim believed
that mechanical solidarity was replaced by an organic type of solidarity.
Here the division of labour itself became a moral force. People were bound
into society by their interdependence. Doctors and fire brigades, and all
other specialised occupations, performed reliably and to the best of their
ability because they knew that any failure on their part could be calami-
tous for others. In turn, they knew that they were dependent on others to
supply goods and services that they could not provide for themselves.

In Durkheim's view, the division of labour was a self-perpetuating
process. Any weakening of the *conscience collective* and mechanical solidarity had to be addressed by a greater division of labour to lessen depend-
ence on mechanical solidarity and to boost organic solidarity, which
further weakened mechanical solidarity, and this cycle would be repeated
again and again.

Durkheim believed that the division of labour could take abnormal,
pathological forms. One was anomie (normlessness), where rules were

non-existent or unclear. Such circumstances were considered likely in times of rapid social change – sharp improvements in living standards as well as severe slumps. Another pathological state was egoism, when individuals could not see how they fitted in and how they were interdependent on others. Durkheim's books included *Suicide* (1897) in which he claimed to show how such incidents rose in times of rapid change (*anomic suicide*), and when individuals were insufficiently integrated (divorced, separated, bereaved or otherwise single rather than married and integrated in families). This was called *egoistic suicide*. A third pathological form was the forced division of labour, where individuals were obliged to play roles for which they were unsuited. Durkheim appears to have believed that a 'hidden hand' would normally allocate everyone to the roles for which they were best equipped. Durkheim also recognised that solidarity could be excessively strong, indicated by *altruistic suicide*, when individuals sacrificed their lives for the good of the group as during warfare, but if everyone became a hero in this way the inevitable outcome would be defeat.

Durkheim believed that a society's justice system could indicate the extent to which solidarity had become less mechanical and more organic – the switch could never become total. In the most complex societies there were crimes that outraged the public who demanded retribution. However, there were also swathes of commercial and civil law where offenders were simply required to make good the damage that they had caused. In such cases the law was restitutive and offenders did not necessarily suffer public opprobrium.

Marx and Durkheim had very different views about the kind of European societies in which they were living. Where Marx saw class divisions, exploitation and conflict; Durkheim saw interdependence. Whereas Durkheim regarded anomie, egoism and the forced division of labour as exceptional, pathological states; Marx believed that the class relationships formed under capitalism inevitably bred alienation. Marx became sociology's classical theorist of conflict; Durkheim came to stand for consensus, integration and order.

That said, Durkheim was anything but a conservative traditionalist or complacent about the society in which he lived, and he was eager, if possible, to show how his science could identify solutions to problems. He had two tentative solutions to the problem of order. Durkheim was a socialist of a certain type; not a Marxist type. He wanted to strengthen 'professional' associations (these were to be a mixture of features of what we regard as *the* professions and trade unions). Individuals would be integrated into occupational (professional) groups, which would be integrated into firms and industries, and thereby into the wider society. During Durkheim's lifetime similar views were being advocated by syndicalists who wanted enterprises to be owned and run by their workforces, and by supporters of worker co-operatives. Later on there were supporters of corporatism (or corporativism) who wanted a Durkheimian type of integration to be implemented top-down, by the state, as happened under Fascism. Durkheim's other hope was that the *conscience collective* would be strengthened by spreading respect for and faith in science. Like many subsequent sociologists, Durkheim regarded religion as a kind of social cement or glue that helped to bind a society. Thus religion was useful, though Durkheim himself was not a believer. He assumed that existing religions would inevitably concede to science, and he hoped that sociology and other sciences would become the replacement for orthodox religions. Comte had a similar aspiration, which was implemented during his life-time in the opening of a small number of positivist churches. Marxists were invariably on the opposite sides of all these ventures and arguments.

By the mid-twentieth century Durkheim's ideas had been incorporated into functionalist theory, the most influential theory in Western sociology at that time. Talcott Parsons (1902–1979) was sociology's most prominent theorist between the 1930s and the 1970s (Parsons, 1937, 1951, 1966). He regarded societies as social systems, with different institutions perform-ing specialist functions, with everything kept in harmony by consensual values that governed all subsystems. Critics were quick to point out that not everything was functional (crime, poverty and unemployment, for example). Functionalist sociologists admitted that particular parts of a whole could be dysfunctional or functionally neutral, while insisting that their framework of ideas enabled the significance of all particular social practices to be established. They were able to insist that certain essential functions (reproduction and socialisation of the population, and economic production, for example) simply had to be performed, and there plainly had to be a minimum of cultural consensus (such as a common language to make communication possible) for any society to endure. Durkheim's abnormal forms of the division of labour became popular (in sociology) explanations of sources of crime and other forms of deviance.

FERDINAND TÖNNIES, THE CHICAGO SCHOOL AND URBANISATION

Both Durkheim and Marx recognised the importance of cities in the construction of modern ways of life. From Durkheim's perspective, popu-lation density and the creation of specialised occupations undermined mechanical solidarity and required the strengthening of organic interde-pendences. For Marx and Engels, the centres of manufacturing and trade which drew together thousands of workers were conducive to the development of class consciousness, solidarity and action. However, these theorists did not identify urbanisation as a master trend that was transforming European societies. Other theorists did bring urbanism to the forefront, but here it is impossible to name a single high-profile founding father of sociology.

If an European is to be nominated it must be Ferdinand Tönnies (1855–1936), Germany's first professional sociologist. His most famous work was titled *Gemeinschaft and Gesellschaft*, translated into English as *Community and Association*, though neither English word conveys the full meaning of the originals (Tönnies, 1887). This book contrasted the village and the city. In villages, families (blood ties) and churches had been at the core of social life. Relationships between villagers were organic (though not in the Durkheimian sense), deep and emotional, whether warm or bitter. Daily life was governed by what Tönnies called 'natural will'. People acted in ways that were customary and which were experienced as natural. Positions were ascribed. Everyone knew their stations in life. There was a presumption of immobility: sons were expected to succeed fathers, and daughters were expected to live as had their mothers. Life was very different in the cities, to which Tönnies was far less warmly disposed. Here relationships were contractual, more formal, governed by 'rational will'. People acted calculatively in their dealings with each other rather than habitually and in ways that seemed just natural. Life was competitive in cities. Positions were achieved. Everyone was expected to strive to get ahead.

Georg Simmel (1858–1918), another German and a contemporary of Tönnies, wrote about the effects of the metropolis on mental life (Simmel, 1903). In cities people would have far more relationships with others than in a rural village, but most urban relationships were superficial. Reserve was an essential protective mechanism. Becoming personally involved with every contact would result in emotional overload. People were dealt with as actors in specific roles rather than as whole persons. An individual would probably really get to know fewer people than in a rural community. Conversely, the city dweller might feel not really understood or valued by anyone. This urban predicament was to be captured in the title of the book, *The Lonely Crowd*, authored by the American sociologist David Riesman and first published in 1952. People could find it necessary to adopt extravagant mannerisms and ostentatious ways of dressing in order to stand out and gain attention.

Social reformers in nineteenth-century Europe were gravely concerned about conditions in the expanding industrial cities. Urbanisation was not leading to increased levels of poverty or higher rates of mortality. On the contrary, on these indicators throughout the century life was getting better. People were migrating from countryside into the cities in search of better lives. However, the cities contained unprecedented concentrations of a variety of problems. Cholera and other epidemics could spread rapidly and affect thousands within weeks. Moreover, cities appeared to be breeding grounds for crime, prostitution and a host of additional depravities. Yet cities had been centres of government, culture and commerce in Europe throughout the Middle Ages. During industrialisation the cities became larger, but their main features were not completely new and therefore startling.

Urbanisation was given greater prominence in North American sociology during its development between the 1890s and the Second World War. Throughout this period the University of Chicago was pre-eminent in American sociology. Its sociology department was founded in 1892, three years ahead of Bordeaux. In 1895 the world's first sociology journal, the *American Journal of Sociology*, was launched from Chicago. The sociological output from Chicago during this period was varied and wide-ranging, but the title 'Chicago School' is attached to the stream of work that used Chicago itself as a quasi-laboratory (see Bulmer, 1984).

America did not produce a series of theorists who worked on the scale of Comte, Marx and Durkheim, taking the whole of human history as their subject matter. The most likely reason is that America did not have a long history. There had been no monarchy, aristocracy, *ancien regime* or feudal relationships to overturn. The settlers from Europe who began to arrive in the sixteenth century were leaving behind such traditions. The 'land of the free' did have African slaves and indigenous Americans, but their positions in colonial America were anything but traditional. The changes experienced in America from the 1890s onwards were all associated with the expansion of the major cities. There was no longer a land frontier in the American west. The main internal population drift was henceforth from rural into urban areas. This was a period of large-scale immigration. The door to America remained open, and the new waves of newcomers were heading for and then remaining in cities such as New York and Chicago. During this same period the American economy was creating large corporations, always based in major cities. Sociologists treated the cities as microcosms of the new America, as in Robert and Helen Lynd's (1929, 1937) successive studies of *Middletown* (actually Muncie), and in William Lloyd Warner and colleagues' studies in *Yankee City* (actually Newburyport in Massachusetts) which were reported in five books between 1941 and 1959 (Warner, 1948, 1949, 1950, 1959; Warner and Lunt, 1941).

There was no equivalent study of Chicago. The Chicago School's output was a series of vignettes of particular districts, occupational and ethnic groups, plus an over-arching theory about city growth. The School's famous ecological model claimed that cities grew and were shaped through competition for space between a variety of groups. The overall outcome was typically a series of concentric bands, the wealthiest residents continuously moving outwards into more spacious suburbs leaving weaker groups in inner-city districts. The weakest of all were said to be found in a 'zone of transition' close to the centre where residential quarters were squeezed for space by businesses and city entertainment. New waves of immigrants moved into these areas, typically accommodated in over-crowded tenements. The districts became infamous for their poor health, high-crime rates, and the low attainments of pupils in the local schools. The districts looked disorganised, chaotic in the eyes of distant observers. Residents came from a variety of places. However, investigators found that the residents were organised informally in a series of subcultures, usually with an ethnic base. There could be Irish, Italian, German, Polish and other quarters. One way for newcomers to get ahead in America was to start businesses, maybe catering for their own local people, or maybe operating on the margins or outside the law in sex, gambling and alcohol during prohibition in America which lasted from 1920 until 1933. There were potentially lucrative occupations awaiting taxi dance hall girls and pool room hustlers. Enterprises in these neighbourhoods usually had to arrange their own protection or come to informal arrangements with the local police and city officials. An outcome was a set of alternative opportunities, ways of initially getting on in America, before gradually moving from the zone of transition, outwards and upwards, to be replaced by new waves of immigrants.

Critics noted that cities did not always grow in concentric circles, and that planning and politics could join market processes in shaping city ecology, but these points did not diminish the influence of the Chicago School. This pioneering work helped to promote the community study into a standard sociological research strategy, and likewise the study of neighbourhood, ethnic and youth subcultures. The investigation of crime and other forms of deviance made a quantum leap by recognising that individuals could be breaking the rules of the wider society through conformity to the informal rules of their local subcultures.

MAX WEBER (1864–1920) AND RATIONALISATION

Weber, another German (clearly with France the main starting-point for European sociology), is the last of the founding fathers. There have been subsequent attempts to join and several nominations, but none have gained all-round recognition as peers of Durkheim, Marx and Weber. Weber might have ended the classical grand style of sociological theorising more abruptly had not most of his work been published gradually over many years following the author's death (see Gerth and Mills, 1946). Most of the books with Weber's name on the spine have been compiled from manuscripts which he left (some clearly incomplete). How Weber would have completed these papers, and drawn everything together, had he lived to do so, have been issues for conjecture and interpretation. The following, like all coherent accounts of Weber's work, is just one 'gloss'.

Weber had a conventional academic career, but he was always engaged in public affairs, and came closer to political power than any of the other founding fathers. He held posts in state administration during and following the First World War. In present-day terms his politics would be labelled centre-left. In 1912 he was part of a group that founded a new (unsuccessful) political party that attempted to merge Germany's Liberals and Social Democrats. Weber never held an academic appointment as a sociologist, though he was recognised as a sociologist by peers (who included Tönnies and Simmel) during his lifetime. Even so, he could equally be claimed by law, economics, history or political science. The boundaries between these disciplines remained weak until the Second World War. Maybe it was best that way!

Weber's intellectual starting-point was different from those of all his predecessors and contemporaries in sociology, partly because Weber seems to have been more knowledgeable about non-European civilisations. The puzzle from which Weber proceeded was why economic growth had taken-off in eighteenth- and nineteenth-century Europe but not elsewhere when material conditions were equally favourable in other parts of the world. Weber's answer was that Protestant religion had been the crucial catalyst in Europe: a catalyst that simply could not have arisen anywhere else. This was the argument in the sole book that Weber published during his lifetime, *The Protestant Ethic and the Spirit of Capitalism* (1905). It was the Protestantism of John Calvin (1509–1564) rather than Martin Luther (1483–1546) that Weber held responsible. Two Calvinist doctrines were considered crucial.

- First, predestination: Calvin preached that the omnipotent and omniscient deity must have predetermined which humans were destined for heaven and hell (a doctrine shared with Mohammed, 570–632 AD, the founder of Islam). Calvin preached that salvation could not be earned during life on earth (by deeds), certainly not through prayer and gifts to a church.

- Second, the calling: people's roles on earth (like their fates following death) were preordained, selected for them by the almighty whose judgement could not be questioned. Work in one's calling was therefore a religious duty. While people could not earn salvation, Calvinists believed that success in one's calling was at least a sign of grace.

Together Weber claimed that these doctrines produced a this-worldly asceticism; people would work energetically and always anxiously in their callings, never feeling that they had done enough, and therefore never able to let-up. If they were successful, they were not earning salvation but simply receiving encouraging signs that they were among the chosen few. In support of this argument Weber marshalled evidence that within Europe capitalism had developed first and most strongly in Protestant rather than Catholic countries, and within Protestant countries among the Calvinist congregations.

Weber did not believe that there was anything novel in capitalists hiring and 'exploiting' labour, or seeking to maximise their profits. What was different post-Reformation was the single-minded, never-ending way in which profit was pursued. Weber believed that Calvinism had been the spark which, amid other favourable conditions (the expansion of trade and industry), had fomented a historically novel rational orientation towards life in general. Once established, the outlook could be routinised. People could be driven by a wholly secular work ethic, but such an ethic could not be created by economic conditions alone. For Weber, the division of labour itself was not a new process; what was novel was the rational approach to splitting work into separate tasks, then bundling these into jobs, and coordinating all operations. A rational outlook made people willing to abandon traditions and customs in favour of whatever way was most efficient and effective. People thought and acted calculatively, in terms of ends and means, and they organised their own lives, and when possible the lives of others as well, according to whatever seemed the best way of achieving their ends.

Entrepreneurs who had never done enough or earned enough, whose businesses never grew large enough to declare 'enough', was just one of the features of the modern world which Weber attributed to the spirit of rationality and a corresponding decline in the influence of tradition. Another outcome was the development of the sciences and the related technologies. It was always possible to learn more and to do things even better. Modern legal codes and practices were said to be further outcomes of rationality: laws that were written down, explicit, to which rulers as well as others were subject, and where there were clear procedures for changing laws. Laws were no longer declared by prophets or bishops, or fixed by tradition. However, the outcome that appears to have concerned Weber most deeply was the spread of bureaucratic administration in large businesses and particularly in departments of state. Weber regarded bureaucracy as a historically novel way of coordinating the work of large armies of employees.

Bureaucracy exemplified modern rationality – coordinating the activities of huge organisations towards a single objective. In a bureaucracy the work to be accomplished is divided into tasks, which are distributed between offices, which are arranged hierarchically, and the work of each office is governed by written rules. People are appointed to offices on the basis of technical competence, certified by qualifications, rather than by patronage or purchase of office, and while performing official duties they are required to set-aside all private interests. Weber believed that legal-rational bureaucracies were social inventions that could mobilise unprecedented power. No single individual would be competent to do everything. Maybe no one would know everything that was happening throughout an organisation. Yet from a command position the work of a huge bureaucracy could be coordinated towards a goal. Large organisations were not new. Europe's monarchs had ruled vast territories and populations. The Romans and the Chinese had built empires. Weber's argument was that bureaucracies were more powerful than regimes that were governed by tradition, and where power was exercised via patrimonial, family-like relationships.

The power of modern bureaucracies was a political issue for Weber, and one reason why he was pessimistic for the future of Europe. He was uncertain whether democratically elected but nevertheless amateur politicians would be able to exert control as opposed to being controlled by their civil services. Was it possible that bureaucratic monsters might spin beyond all human control? The fears must have strengthened when Europe's politicians were unable to prevent the continent marching into a First World War that, it was said, none of the continent's politicians really wanted.

Why had there been a religious Reformation and all that followed in the West but not in India or China? Weber's work included studies of these countries' religions. His conclusion was that a Western-type Reformation was possible only within the occidental religions that had evolved from Judaism, in which God was outside the world, but able to speak to the people through prophets. This simply could not happen in Hinduism, Buddhism, Taoism or Confucianism. However, this did not prevent these countries adopting Western practices when imposed by imperial powers, or by choice as following the Meiji Restoration in Japan in 1868.

From all contemporary accounts, Weber was deeply pessimistic about the future of Europe, and not only through fears of bureaucratic machines taking over or falling into the hands of dictators. He did not regard socialism as a solution but rather as a way in which rationalisation might be extended further. Weber was pessimistic about the disenchantment that he saw spreading all around. Rationalisation made everything predictable and drained life of excitement. People were locked into social arrangements that embraced them as powerfully as if they were iron cages. People were safe, relieved of responsibility, and bored! George Ritzer (1993), the present-day American sociologist, believes that rationalisation is currently spreading from government and manufacturing into consumption and consumer services, a process that he calls 'McDonaldization', which threatens to make leisure boring.

CONCLUSIONS

Marx, Durkheim, Weber, Tönnies and the urban studies pioneered in Chicago remain fixtures on all sociology syllabuses because the trends that each of them highlighted – the growth of capitalism, the division of labour, urbanisation and rationalisation – have still not been reversed or ended: all are ongoing. However, after 1945 the Western world was experiencing a new set of transformative changes which enlarged sociology's agenda. Also, as explained in later chapters in this book, after 1945 European and American sociology converged. America was introduced to European theory. Simultaneously, European sociology embraced and incorporated America's (specifically Chicago's) practice of undertaking detailed studies of contemporary social conditions.

3. Twentieth-century transformations

INTRODUCTION

Europe, 1914–1945

Current sociology has little to tell its students about this period. Maybe this is because its sociology produced no great theories or names that have remained on syllabuses alongside Marx, Durkheim and Weber. Modern history (as represented in sociology) leaps from nineteenth-century industrialisation and urbanisation straight into the late-1940s.

The big events that occurred between 1914 and 1945 were not predicted by sociology's founding fathers. The general expectation among Europe's intellectuals towards the end of the nineteenth century was that modern societies would become more peaceful and prosperous. In the event, twentieth-century Europe produced two world wars that required the conscription of males of fighting age and the mobilisation of civilian populations. Economic conditions were harsh in continental Europe throughout the 1920s. In the 1930s the economies of Europe and North America sank into the Great Depression. Unemployment and poverty were widespread. New political movements gathered strength in Europe, foremost the Fascist movements that by 1939 were in power in Italy, Austria, Germany, Spain and Portugal, and also arguably in Poland, Yugoslavia, Bulgaria and the three Baltic states (Estonia, Latvia and Lithuania). Fascism was aggressively anti-intellectual, so the movements have not left a philosophy that would assist us today in understanding their appeal. All the Fascist parties were virulently anti-Communist, they were nationalist, believed that nations were best represented by single political parties, and that all other associations from businesses and trade unions to churches and boy scouts should be subordinate to the state. Sociology students may learn about Germany's Nazi (national socialist) variant of Fascism and the Holocaust, but not about the more widespread appeal and achievements of Fascism. Yet these systems might have become the future of Europe had not Germany and its allies been defeated by the Soviet army.

There had been a Bolshevik Revolution in Russia in 1917, during the First World War, at a point when Russia's armed forces were in retreat.

After having rejoined in time to be among the victors in the war, Russia's self-described Marxist regime took control of the former Tsarist Empire (except the Baltic states). Marx had predicted the eventual success of socialist parties, but Russia was not among the places where initial success was anticipated. Nevertheless, the Russian Bolsheviks consolidated power at home, took on and triumphed over the German army in the Second World War, and after 1945 their Soviet system was extended into South-East and East-Central Europe. Communism was on the march and its supporters believed that history was on their side. After 1989 this system became history. The entire history of Communism, like Fascism, can now be bracketed off as a historical digression, the countries having rejoined the modern mainstream. A common view today is that all countries are now situated at different points in a global modernisation process. History did not have to turn out this way. Between the First World War and 1989 there were competing versions of modern industrial society. In another 50 years there may be different Western, Islamic, Asian, Russian and African versions. However, the course of history up to the present can be treated as justification for Western sociology, since 1945, drawing its main issues from the changes in its home countries. By the 1950s these were becoming social market economies, welfare states and social democracies.

The Transformation of Sociology

By the end of the 1950s sociology was becoming part of the standard university offer throughout Western Europe and North America, but it was a different kind of sociology than had been developed and taught (in far fewer places) before the Second World War. Auguste Comte had coined the term, and in Europe 'sociology' was subsequently reserved for social theories with a long historical sweep.

There was another kind of social science that developed in nineteenth-century Europe, and as explained in Chapter 2, from the 1890s onwards in North America also (where it was called sociology). This involved collecting facts about the condition of the people. During the nineteenth century all governments in the industrialising countries began to undertake regular censuses of their populations, and to collect data on births, marriages and deaths. In Britain government inspectors examined and reported on conditions in coal mines and factories, and public health commissions investigated conditions in the industrial towns. By the 1890s Charles Booth in London and Seebohm Rowntree in York were conducting their famous investigations into the extent and causes of poverty. This kind of social research was closely allied to reform movements. It was believed that once the facts about social conditions became generally known, then action

and improvement would surely follow. Voluntary associations, sometimes linked to churches, which aimed to alleviate poverty and to improve
health, housing and family life (the pioneers of twentieth-century social
work), often prided themselves on the 'scientific' basis of their efforts.
When this kind of social science was made into an academic subject in
Europe, it was called social science or social administration (a title later
dropped in favour of social policy). This was separate and distinct from
European sociology prior to the Second World War.

After 1945 Western sociology embraced fact gathering. American sociology, pioneered at Chicago, had always investigated social conditions.
European social theory was injected into American sociology between
the world wars, largely through the efforts of Talcott Parsons whose
first book, *The Structure of Social Action* (1937), was an account and
attempted synthesis of the ideas of Europe's main social theorists. We
can note that Karl Marx did not feature in this book. The Italian theorist,
Vilfredo Pareto (1848–1923), was prominent, but he has not survived as a
recognised founding father. If referred to today, Pareto is most likely to
be identified as an elite theorist along with Gaetano Mosca (1858–1941)
and Robert Michels (1876–1936). These writers considered rule by elites
to be inevitable, albeit for somewhat different reasons, and their arguments seemed plausible during the rise of Fascism and the development of
Marxism into Marxism-Leninism then Stalinism.

By the 1950s there was broad agreement on both sides of the Atlantic
that sociology should encompass both theory and research. Theories were
to be properly grounded in evidence, and research was to be theoretically
relevant as well as useful to policymakers and social workers. Robert K.
Merton, an American sociologist, advocated the development of 'theories of the middle range' which would bridge Europe's broad sweeps of
history and fact-gathering (Merton, 1949). In *The Sociological Imagination*
(1959), C. Wright Mills, another American sociologist, lambasted abstract
theory on the one side (with Talcott Parsons at the centre of the criticisms)
together with fact collecting for its own sake. Wright Mills wanted a sociology that would convert private troubles into public issues, like showing
how one person's unemployment was part of a wider problem created by
the character of the socio-economic system.

A problem with Merton's 'middle range' was that Europe's theories of
history were really too sweeping to be 'tested' in any type of investigation.
Thus these theories became not a source of hypotheses to test, but alternative or complementary frameworks of ideas, ways of thinking about
specific issues that researchers could investigate, and the issues that mainstream sociology addressed from the 1950s onwards were mostly about the
transformations that were perceived to be underway in Western countries.

SOCIAL DEMOCRACY

The Social Market Economy

Anyone who experienced the world wars and life in the 1920s and 1930s, and who lived into the 1950s, could hardly but feel that a new era had dawned. Full employment was achieved as Europe's and North America's economies recovered from war and re-geared to peacetime markets. The economies grew steadily for '30 glorious years' at a rate unequalled before or since in the West. Workers achieved year-on-year increases in real wage levels, which spread prosperity throughout the populations. Commentators began to write about an affluent society with affluent workers. Britain's voters did not need Harold Macmillan, Conservative Prime Minister from 1957 to 1963, to tell them that they had 'never had it so good'.

The transformation in economic conditions was largely due to the widespread acceptance and implementation of policies recommended by the Cambridge economist, John Maynard Keynes (1883–1946). He had argued that governments could smooth-out business cycles which created booms and slumps, achieve steady economic growth and maintain full employment by countervailing against market forces. This meant that when an economy was contracting, the government should inject money into consumers' wallets (by cutting taxes and maybe raising the pay of its own employees), and spending more on public works. When an economy boomed the government should do the reverse. These policies worked, and meant that governments became responsible for economic management in wider senses than simply balancing their own books and protecting the value of national currencies. In Europe governments extended their leverage by taking major industries into public ownership. The strengthening of welfare states (see below) also meant that governments themselves accounted for enlarged shares of their national economies. Governments consulted trade unions and federations of employers on matters of economic management. The outcome was called a social market economy. The economies were mixtures of private and public sectors. Private businesses continued to pursue profits for their owners, but within a policy framework which meant that in doing so they were serving their societies rather than just their shareholders.

The apparent success of social markets led to Europe's main political parties of the left abandoning the aim of taking entire economies into public ownership. In the UK, the Labour politician Anthony Crosland (1956) argued that ownership had become irrelevant: privately and publicly owned enterprises could equally serve the public interest. In 1943

James Burnham, an American political theorist, had argued that power in businesses was slipping out of the hands of owners into the hands of a rising class of managers, a so-called managerial revolution. By the 1960s the orthodox view was represented by John Kenneth Galbraith (1908–2006), an American economist, who was arguing that managers and professionals could run publicly and privately owned organisations in accordance with objectives agreed by owners, workers and governments (Galbraith, 1967).

Welfare States

In 1942 Sir William Beveridge (1879–1963) chaired a committee and wrote its report to the UK government which became the basis of Britain's post-war welfare state, constructed initially by the Labour governments of 1945–1951. Beveridge was an economist, and at different times a civil servant, academic and Liberal politician. His report identified five evils that had blighted pre-war Britain: idleness, poverty, disease, ignorance and squalor. By the early-1950s all had either been conquered or were perceived as en route to extinction. The foundations of welfare states (the adopted term) that were built in Britain and other Western countries were:

- Full employment.
- The full range of educational opportunities open to children whatever their social origins.
- Health care free at the point of use, according to need.
- A right to decent housing.
- Income maintenance for vulnerable groups and for everyone at vulnerable points in the life course, which meant child benefits, maternity grants, unemployment and sickness pay, support for the long-term incapacitated and retirement pensions: in other words, security from the cradle to the grave.

By the early-1950s Britain could claim to have the world's strongest welfare state, but in this respect, and in standards of living, Britain was soon being overtaken by continental European countries. By the 1960s Sweden and other Scandinavian countries were building, and have retained to the present day, Europe's and indeed the world's strongest state welfare regimes.

The USA can be regarded as an exception to much of the above. America did not take major industries into public ownership. Health care has remained a mixture of private insurance, charity and public assistance. Apart from retirement pensions (called social security in America), income maintenance provisions have varied from state to state. Fees have always been charged in higher education. However, it is probably best to regard the USA as developing its own version of a social market, and creating its own kind of welfare state. America's *New Deal* public works programmes in the 1930s were among the pioneering steps in Keynesian economic management. In the 1960s the federal government launched a *War on Poverty* in a bid to create a *Great Society*. These measures were in part responses to the civil rights movement that was demanding an end to racial segregation and discrimination, and genuine equal opportunities.

In 1990 the Danish sociologist, Gosta Esping-Andersen, identified three types of capitalist welfare states, subsequently extended to four.

- Social-democratic: highly decommodified and universal benefits (the best examples are the Scandinavian countries). Decommmodified means that services are not marketed as commodities. So provision does not depend on profitability, and access does not depend on ability and willingness to pay.
- Conservative-corporatist: high decommodification but benefits are not universal – they depend on type of occupation and contributions paid (France and Germany are examples).
- Liberal: highly commodified with means-tested benefits for the needy (as in the USA).
- A fourth type of regime, where welfare is left primarily to the family, may be added (Southern European countries being examples).

Using this typology, the UK was once a mixture of the social-democratic and conservative types, but has subsequently moved in a liberal direction.

Social Democracy and Industrial Society

Social democracy was the name given to the societies created by the management of social markets and the construction of welfare states. The political momentum was from parties of the left, but the reforms became consensual. Social democracy became the political centre ground. The working classes had organised themselves in trade unions, which had created socialist political parties, as Marx had envisaged, but rather than seeking revolutions that would overthrow capitalism, these parties had chosen the 'parliamentary, democratic' road, and settled for reforming capitalism – transforming free markets into social markets, and using the wealth generated to pay higher wages to workers and to fund welfare states. The success of social democracy in the West after 1945 resulted in recruitment to the expanding political forces of the inter-war years – Communists and Fascists – shrivelling to a trickle.

Sociology was not the source of the thinking that led, and it was not in the lead in constructing the social market, welfare states or social democracy. A feature of sociology since its nineteenth-century origins has been that major work recognised as sociological has often been produced by people who were not formally qualified or employed as sociologists. The post-war transformations were planned and theorised mainly by economists, political scientists and policy experts (from the kind of social science that was assimilated into post-war sociology). One of sociology's most prominent theoretical contributions was by the American Daniel Bell (1960) who proclaimed an 'end of ideology'. His claim was that the battle of big ideas, capitalism versus socialism, was over, and that the new politics was about means rather than ends: who could manage the social market and welfare state most competently. Bell sided with certain American economists (Galbraith, 1967; Kerr et al., 1960) who were predicting a convergence between Communist and Western societies. At that time, in the 1950s and 1960s, the Soviet authorities were injecting some market processes into their centrally planned, command economy. An extension of these developments alongside further strengthening of state planning in the West was to produce convergence. Communism and capitalism were reconceptualised as alternative routes into the industrial age, or as alternative ways of running an advanced industrial society, rather than entirely different systems. In the event there was to be no convergence: the Communist systems disappeared after 1989.

The Post-scarcity Generation and New Social Movements

An unplanned outcome of the social democracy package was the formation of a new generation with the baby boomers (the name given to the cohorts born during the high birth rate years that followed the Second World War) in the vanguard. The American sociologist, Ronald Inglehart (1977) identified how they differed from people who had experienced the 1930s and the Second World War. The baby boomers took freedom from the threats of poverty and unemployment for granted. They grew up assuming that they would live better lives than their parents (at least in material terms). They did not grow up being prepared for war. Their main demand, which they simply enacted, was for greater personal freedom. The outcomes were new flamboyant youth cultures, a hit parade and fashions dictated by teenagers' tastes, and especially when the contraceptive pill became available during the 1960s, greater sexual freedom. The working-class youth cultures of the 1950s were joined by a new kind of student culture in the 1960s. Sherry parties were out; recreational drugs and sex were in. Students were in the vanguard of new socio-political movements; for peace, race and gender quality, and later-on environmental issues. Students in the USA lined up with the civil rights (for African-Americans) movement, and led protests against America's involvement in the Vietnam War. In Europe the protests evolved into attacks on the entire post-war system; the still basically capitalist economy, state power, university government, in fact the entire military-economic-political-educational complex. Protests on the streets of Paris in 1968, when students were joined by workers, threatened the French government. Clearly, the upcoming generation was not at ease with post-war Western society.

Sociology Appraises Social Democracy

Sociology (as practised at the time) may not have produced any of the really big ideas, but the European (and North American) fact gathering social researchers who were to be embraced by post-1945 Western sociology had documented the pre-war conditions to which the post-war reforms were a response. They had studied the effects of unemployment on individuals, families and communities, and measured the prevalence of poverty, chronic ill-health and squalid housing. From the 1950s onwards an expanding and vibrant sociology was using social science research tools to appraise the achievements and limitations of social democracy. Nearly all sociologists had personally been on the side of social reform. They were pro-social democracy unless their views were further to the left. Their post-war research assessed the achievements of social democracy and usually queried whether the social-democratic reforms had gone far enough or whether further reform was needed, or whether a real step change in social conditions needed more radical measures than social democracy could accommodate.

First, the core issue in sociology in the 1950s and 1960s was how people's lives were being changed (and improved) by full employment, the welfare state, rising real wages and standards of living. A series of studies, the most famous of which being in Britain, Michael Young and Peter Willmott's *Family and Kinship in East London* (1957), highlighted changes in family and neighbourhood life. Nuclear family households were becoming less dependent on the support of kin and neighbours. Husbands were playing a larger role in childcare: some were prepared to be seen pushing prams! Homes were more comfortable and were being equipped with television sets. Changes in family and community life accelerated when residents from inner-city slums were rehoused on suburban estates or (more bleakly) in high-rise developments. These investigations alerted a wider public to what was being lost. Popular television programmes such as the UK's long-running *Coronation Street* illustrate how nostalgia for what was really a much grimmer past has remained prevalent into the twenty-first century.

Second, by the end of the 1940s government statistics were showing that poverty was fast disappearing as a result of full employment, rising real wages and state welfare. The poverty that had all but disappeared was subsistence poverty – lacking the resources necessary for physical survival. By the 1960s some sociologists were arguing (and they won this argument) that a subsistence definition was inappropriate in more affluent societies. They proposed defining poverty in relative terms – lacking the resources to lead a decent life, as defined by the general public at the time. Researchers were able to discover what were considered essentials in order to live decently. They could measure how far below the median income households had to fall before they were obliged to go without these decencies. The effect of this redefinition was the rediscovery of poverty, and evidence that, far from vanishing, poverty was actually becoming more widespread and severe, mainly due to welfare benefits failing to keep pace with increases in earned incomes (Abel-Smith and Townsend, 1966). This argument was won in the sense that national governments throughout the West now define and measure poverty in terms of how many households fall below 60 per cent or 70 per cent of the median income, moderated for household composition. Large numbers of children being reared in poverty (around one in six in Britain in the early twenty-first century) is considered particularly unacceptable.

Third, the quality of working life became another new issue, or rather an old issue that had not gone away. Workers were being paid more. Working hours had been reduced. Nevertheless, research showed that work could be as alienating as ever. *The Man on the Assembly Line* was a book title (Walker and Guest, 1952) and emblematic of the kind of employment that was being created in the industries that produced the consumer goods to be purchased by affluent workers.

Fourth, class divisions at work were shown to be as stark as ever. There was a debate within and beyond sociology in the 1950s and 1960s about whether affluence was leading to the embourgeoisement of the working class, that is, their assimilation into the middle class. The unequivocal verdict from research was that the post-war working class might be better paid, but it was still working class. Its members' lives at work and outside remained separate and different from those of their managers, and the workers retained working-class identities and political proclivities (see Goldthorpe et al., 1969).

Fifth, post-war researchers found that the link between children's social class origins and their attainments in education remained strong. This was probably post-war sociology's least expected and most startling finding. Life chances in the welfare state were still highly dependent on the class into which a child was born. The rate of relative social mobility did not appear to have changed since the early-twentieth century. Thus social democracy had evidently failed to equalise opportunities (Goldthorpe et al., 1980; Halsey et al., 1980; Jackson and Marsden, 1962).

Additional inequalities were being made into public issues by post-war sociology (fulfilling C. Wright Mills' aspiration for sociology). Gender was promoted as an issue in sociology and in the wider society by second-wave feminism. Race had been a long-standing issue in the USA and it was becoming a new issue in European countries that were experiencing rising levels of immigration from former colonies (see Chapter 5).

Before the Second World War social scientists had investigated how many people lived beneath or just on the poverty line, social inequalities in rates of morbidity and mortality, the proportions of dwellings without indoor plumbing, and how children's education was restricted by financial barriers. After the war sociology reframed these issues. It examined relative inequalities, the social and cultural as well as the material aspects of inequality at work, in standards and styles of living, and in terms of the uses that different socio-demographic groups made of nominally equal educational opportunities. Sociology also asked how these inequalities were best explained: in terms of the functions that they performed for society as a whole, as outcomes of capitalism, or of divisions present in all industrial societies that were most likely to continue under full strength socialism (see Chapter 4). The verdict on social democracy was that everyone had moved up as a result of economic growth, full employment and state welfare, but without necessarily even reducing inequalities.

All the above have remained issues in sociology into the twenty-first century, but the present-day context is different. Until the 1970s the debate was about whether further progress could be made within social democracy. If not, then full socialism was surely inevitable. In the UK Ralph Miliband (1969, 1973) argued that the 'parliamentary road' and reform could deliver little while the economy remained basically capitalist. He argued that under these circumstances governments of the left had no real choice but to prioritise the interests of capital.

Maybe post-war sociology was over-harsh in its verdicts on social democracy. It was critical of how wide economic inequalities remained, the extent to which life chances remained governed by birth, and that work remained alienating even when industries had been taken into public ownership. Maybe sociology in the 1950s and 1960s was under-appreciative of the ways in which full employment, the welfare state and rising real wage levels had removed not just the experience but the threat of subsistence poverty. However, we must bear in mind that sociologists' judgements were within an expectation that if social democracy had delivered too little, popular pressure would eventually lead either to its extension and strengthening or an even more radical change of system.

Social democracy was sometimes described as a 'settlement' under which capitalism paid a price for retaining wealth in private hands, and allowing a capitalist class to own and run businesses and make profits. At that time, few in sociology or on the political left thought it likely, or even possible, that capitalism might decide that the price was too high. The issue up until the 1970s was how much further towards full socialism societies should move, and how rapidly. The assumption was that the working classes in Western societies could force further change if they wished – they were majorities of the populations. However, over the next 30 years capital was to demonstrate that it did not need to pay forever higher wages but could gain workers' compliance with the return of the threat of unemployment, and by exposing Western workforces to competition from lower wage cost, newly industrialising countries. Managers and professionals were about to be shown that their careers depended not on serving a wider public interest but on putting profits and share prices ahead of all other considerations.

POST-INDUSTRIAL SOCIETY

It is easiest to label and list an era's main characteristics when it has become history or at least peaked, like the post-war age of social democracy. There are numerous labels for the era that has followed: information age, knowledge economy, network society, high modernity, late modernity, modernity II, post-modern. Post-industrial is a label with which no one is likely to quarrel. Its meaning is well understood and consensual, and there is no dispute that this is among the changes that make the present different from the decades that immediately followed the Second World War. Among sociologists there is little dissent from the view that the age of building social democracies is now in the past, even though many of its achievements live on and some are being extended.

- Governments have been abandoning Keynesian economic management. Monetarism, a set of doctrines advocated by the American economist Milton Friedman (1981), has become influential. There has been a shift away from corporatist economic management in favour of deregulation. Supporters of these developments are called neo-liberals, after the original nineteenth-century 'Manchester' liberals who advocated free trade as part of their wider support for free markets.

- Welfare states have been rolled back rather than strengthened.
- The old social-democratic centre-left is no longer the political centre ground. This has shifted to somewhere right of centre-right. Former social-democratic parties have changed their policies (rightwards), usually without changing the parties' names.

Politics

Politicians who dominated the 1980s in Britain and the USA became icons of the arrival of new times. Margaret Thatcher, UK Prime Minister from 1979–1990, and Ronald Reagan, US President from 1981–1989, were soulmates, impressed by the ideas of the economist Milton Friedman who argued that the money supply, managed to keep inflation low, should be the key lever of economic policy, and that markets should be left to set levels of employment (and unemployment). Both were Cold War warriors. Reagan condemned the Soviet Union as an evil empire. Margaret Thatcher was known as the Iron Maiden. Both believed in a smaller state. Reagan ended measures introduced in the 1960s as part of the USA's *War on Poverty* together with positive action measures that had been designed to compensate for centuries of discrimination and to accelerate the advance of African-Americans. America was introduced to *Workfare* (claimants working for their benefits). Later on Americans learnt about tough love and time-limited benefits. Both Thatcher and Reagan advocated 'law and order', tougher sentences for convicted criminals, and expanded their countries' prison populations. Margaret Thatcher privatised a series of nationalised industries – oil, gas, electricity, water, telecommunications, air transport and coal mining. She deregulated the labour market by limiting the power of trade unions. She deregulated financial markets in a 'big bang' in 1986 which allowed foreign institutions to trade in London, and abolished 'firewalls' between different kinds of institutions – stock jobbers and stockbrokers, retail banks and building societies, and retail banks and investment banks, for example. An outcome was that London became the world's main financial centre and 'the City' expanded beyond its traditional square mile. Before long New York and Tokyo were deregulating in order to compete with London. The USA, which had never developed as strong a welfare state as European countries, became a model to emulate in Britain. This meant UK versions of *Workfare* policies (which had succeeded in reducing the number of claimants in America), and enlarged roles for private finance in health care and higher education, for example.

Anyone who experienced life before and after the 1980s in Britain or America knew that times had changed. The Second World War had been a similar watershed. Needless to say, as happened after 1945, before long new generations were arriving who treated the new conditions simply as normal.

In 1983 Stuart Hall and Martin Jacques, prominent left-wing intellectuals in the UK, declared that 'new times' had arrived and that the working class could no longer be expected to become a revolutionary force. In 1987 the UK sociologists Scott Lash and John Urry announced the end of organised capitalism. At the end of the 1980s the Communist regimes were swept from power in East-Central and South-East Europe, and in 1991 the Soviet Union broke up and all the new independent states became post-Communist. History was no longer on the side of the left. Political events and personalities were the public faces of the changes, but they were responding to new conditions that have arguably been the real change drivers. Social democracy was a political project, implemented by governments that were guided by a coherent set of ideas and a vision of a better future. The shift into a post-industrial age has been different. Governments and politicians have reacted to global historical forces. There has been no vision of a 'new Jerusalem' towards which we are heading. Hence, as in the nineteenth century, one of sociology's problems has been to identify the drivers of change.

Drivers of Change

First, by the 1970s social democracy was creating problems to which it had no solutions. One was the rising cost of state welfare. This was partly due to population ageing, leading to greater demands on health services and pension funds. Independently of demography, advances in medical science were creating new and expensive treatments for a wide range of conditions. The costs of education were also rising as more young people opted to complete upper secondary (15–18 years) education and then progress into tertiary education. All this was in a context where income taxes were becoming unpopular among workers on average and below average incomes whose contributions were needed. Taxing the rich alone would no longer cover governments' expenses. Employers' profits were also being squeezed whether by the need to concede trade unions' wage demands or by higher contributions to state budgets. This was at a time when Western firms were facing increasing competition from a group of new industrialising countries. Thus employers were seeking an escape from the post-war settlement.

Second, a new generation of technology was becoming available, namely the information and communication technologies (ICT). This was a result of the advent of silicon chips and micro-computing. Before long the new technology was everywhere. It has affected every industry and most occupations within them. Today it is hard to find an office without a desktop computer. Laptops and netbooks enable managers and professionals to carry the office with them wherever they go. The new technology has automated many manufacturing processes, car repair and servicing operations, retailing, banking, and in restaurants waiters can now transmit orders to the kitchen electronically. An outcome has invariably been labour saving, but the other side of this coin has been the development of new industries producing hardware, software including search engines, online shops and interactive sites. New dot.com businesses have been created, and some of their creators have become millionaires. At the beginning of this new technological age it was claimed that an outcome would be a knowledge economy, demanding highly educated workers, who would be employed in high value added, highly skilled, high salary jobs. We now know that such optimistic forecasts neglected the scope for digital Taylorisation (named after Frederick Winslow Taylor, the pioneer of time-and-motion study, so-called scientific management, and the assembly line). The new technology makes it possible to break down much craft and professional work into routine tasks that can be supervised by technology. The optimistic forecasts also failed to envisage the global expansion of higher education which has made highly educated labour plentiful (and often cheap) in all world regions.

Globalisation has been the third change driver. This refers to the increased international flows of capital, goods, services, people and information. Globalisation has occurred partly because the trend has been encouraged by national governments. Most are at least nominally in favour of lowering and eventually eliminating tariffs and other trade barriers. Free trade is supposed to benefit all parties. Economics has a doctrine of comparative advantage which explains how international competition results in all countries specialising in activities where their comparative advantage is greatest, or where their comparative disadvantage is lowest. At the same time, all governments want to protect certain economic sectors: usually agriculture and certain types of mineral extraction and manufacturing in richer countries, and new manufacturing and service sectors in poorer countries. International flows of information and electronic money are probably beyond the control of national governments though some try to block local access to unwelcome Internet sites. Manuel Castells (1996), a Spanish sociologist, has argued that ICT is leading to the formation of a global network society in which organisational and national borders dissolve. Governments today are likely to feel that they have no alternative but to try to insert their countries into global markets by fostering national competitiveness. This may mean attracting investors with offers of low taxes on businesses and offering labour that is highly qualified, skilled, compliant and/or cheap. They may hope that exposure to international competition will force home-based businesses to sharpen their competitive edge. One aspect of globalisation has been the growth of transnational corporations that can base certain operations in countries where labour is cheapest, and take profits where taxes are lowest.

A fourth change driver, operating in tandem with globalisation, has been the financialisation of capitalism. There are still businesses that are owned and controlled by a specific person or group, but most investment is now by financial intermediaries – banks, investment funds, pension funds, insurance companies, unit trusts and so on. They move capital in search of short-term capital gains through movements in share, commodity or currency prices, and medium-term profits. Most transactions in these markets are speculative, that is, seeking a better return, rather than new investment or withdrawals of capital for consumption. Money flows electronically between firms, industries, business sectors and countries 24/7 because markets are always open somewhere on nearly every day of the year. Financial institutions have become key hubs in the global economy. They are able, subject to regulations in the countries where they are based, to create money (credit). Thus today's economic booms which eventually bust are not the result of the over-production of goods (as in Marx's lifetime) but over-lending and over-borrowing. This creates 'bubbles' in asset prices (shares and houses, for example). The bubbles always pop at some point, and in 2008 the world learnt that major financial institutions may need to be rescued (bailed out) by governments (tax-payers) in order to prevent catastrophic economic collapse. Governments (mainly China and some Middle Eastern states) which have retained ownership of national assets (usually mineral resources) have been able to accumulate substantial sovereign wealth funds which can be lent to debtor countries and/ or used to purchase businesses in other countries. Financialisation and globalisation have made it necessary for national governments to create and empower transnational institutions – the European Union, the World Bank, the International Monetary Fund, the World Trade Organisation, and the G7/8/20 (meetings of leaders of the world's major economies) so that businesses can operate globally according to rules. As ever, free markets need rules (laws) so that business transactions can be made with confidence.

Sociology is struggling to engage with current change drivers. This is partly because the societies on which sociology has concentrated up to now have been countries. We need to develop equivalent expertise on international relations. Also, researchers have tended to 'look down' at the poor, the working classes, and no higher than the middle classes. Sociology needs equivalent skill in 'looking up' at the seriously rich and the institutions that manage capital. These have been driving us into the post-industrial age.

Outcomes

First, Sociology is interested in the change drivers and equally in the outcomes. One outcome has been wider economic inequalities. New global rich have been created – bankers, dot.com and other entrepreneurs, company directors and beneficiaries of 'honest robbery' privatisations in the new market economies – who can place their personally held wealth in the most tax friendly places. National governments may feel helpless. They either impose low taxes or receive no taxes. The gap between the highest and the lowest incomes has widened dramatically, and managers and professionals who act on behalf of the seriously wealthy have received pay rises that lift them well above median incomes.

Another change, part of the same transformation, has been the creation of new 'excluded groups' or 'underclasses'. The labels are most appropriate for migrants who are unable to obtain regular, official jobs, who have no welfare rights, nor the right to vote in the countries where they live (temporarily or permanently). These groups are physically 'in' yet apart from the relevant societies. However, other non-migrant groups have been 'excluded' as jobs have been lost and not replaced in the places where they live, and as the protection of welfare states has weakened. The package of changes currently underway simultaneously increases the number of claimants (mainly the retired and the unemployed) while governments seek to reduce their welfare spending.

Second, the outcome from which the latest transformation takes its most popular name (post-industrial) has been the de-industrialisation of the workforces in Western countries. This has been a result of labour saving technologies and the transfer of much manufacturing to lower wage countries. Manufacturing output has declined less steeply, and has not declined at all in the UK, but employment in manufacturing has fallen sharply. Nowadays the original industrial countries have less than 20 per cent of their workforces employed in manufacturing and extractive industries. Employment in service sectors has expanded, and total employment has grown rather than diminished. This is the sense in which the societies have become post-industrial. The loss of manufacturing jobs has been one source of the new unemployment. Maybe as many new jobs have been created as have been lost, but the new jobs are not necessarily in the same places, and are unlikely to be seeking the skills that displaced coal miners and factory workers can offer.

Third, alongside this shift of employment from manufacturing to services, there has been a shift from employment in manual towards non-manual occupations. Manufacturing firms today employ far fewer people in production, but are likely to employ more scientists, technologists, accountants, sales staff and managers. Service sectors employ manual workers in hotels, restaurants, cleaning and security businesses, and hospitals and universities employ porters and cleaners as well as doctors and professors, but overall the service sectors have mainly non-manual workforces. The outcome has been the manual working classes shrinking to become minorities of the populations. The original social bases of trade unions and left-wing political parties have shrunk. The parties' choice, as most have perceived it, has been permanent opposition or change.

Fourth, however, it is the impact of the new times on everyday life that has been responsible for the plethora of labels. New technologies have changed how we work, and how we live the rest of our lives. Micro-technologies help to operate our washers, microwaves and cars. They enable us to use mobile phones, to have multichannel television and the Internet, enabling us to receive information (images, news, music, entertainment) and to be in touch with personally known and virtual friends, as well as living a second life in virtual reality, at any time of the day or night. We now live in a culture-rich, mediated world. Jean Baudrillard (1998), a French sociologist, has speculated on the implications. The world that we feel we know is often in fact a world constructed from media messages and images, sometimes images of images, which Baudrillard calls *simulacra*, which are created when media report and repeat each other's messages. An outcome is said to be a *hyper-reality* in which the media are no longer mediators but actually construct what we take to be reality. Thus the environment in which we live no longer consists primarily of people who are seen and heard directly, who can be touched and thereby confirmed as real. The same applies to places that we think we know and events that we believe have happened.

It is only since the mid-1990s that children have grown up amid what is now the full range of new technologies – digital games, multichannel TV, mobile phones-plus and the Internet. It is probably still far too early to draw conclusions about long-term effects. Electricity was available well before the end of the nineteenth century, but at that time no one envisaged all the products in people's homes that would be electrically powered by the 1930s. New technologies have changed the ways in which young people obtain, store and listen to recorded music. In what ways is the music itself being changed? Are new ways of communicating adding a new dimension to old types of social relationships or wholly or partly replacing them with new networks?

Fifth, a parallel trend has been an explosion in consumption – spending on non-essentials, mainly travel, out-of-home eating and drinking, fashion clothing, sports clothing and footwear, the media and other forms of entertainment. Not everyone is part of this new consumer society. As explained above, economic inequalities have widened. It is mainly the middle classes – those in the better paid jobs, members of their families, and people who expect middle-class careers (students) – who have been behind the boom in consumption. This boom has led to speculation about consumption-based identities replacing occupation-based identities (Miles, 1998), though the ability to consume depends on earning the necessary resources. Meanwhile, the poor are doubly stigmatised – unwanted in the labour market and flawed consumers (Bauman, 1998).

Sixth, some sociologists claim that our society and our lives have become liquid or plastic (see Bauman, 2006). This means different things in different sections of the population. It may refer to affluent consumers who can experiment with different lifestyles. These include many young people and also the so-called 'Woopies' (well-off older people). The young may experience serial sexual partnerships, surrounded by constantly evolving networks of friends, mostly temporary relationships in a world where nothing is for keeps, and they may build careers as they move from job-to-job, extending their skills, and entering each new accomplishment on a lengthening CV. There is another kind of liquidity experienced by those whose former occupations and industries have disappeared, forcing them into or preventing them ever progressing beyond low paid, temporary and part-time jobs in call centres, fast food outlets, supermarkets and suchlike. The world in which they or their parents once made real, tangible goods, and worked indefinitely in occupations and for firms that could offer security, continues to exist only as a folk memory.

Ulrich Beck (1992), a German sociologist, claims that we now live in *risk societies*, a product of modernisation with science and technology having created new risks which we cannot control such as the threat of nuclear disaster, climate change and other ecological calamities. Simultaneously, globalisation (as discussed above) has weakened the ability of national governments to control the forces that are reshaping their own societies. At the same time, the latest modernising trends have involved an acceleration of what Anthony Giddens (1991), a UK sociologist, calls *detraditionalisation* – the weakening of neighbourhoods and religious communities along with extended families. Giddens and Beck concur that an outcome is *individualisation* with personal biographies ceasing to be structured by class, gender and local job opportunities. Individuals are thus forced to become reflexive and to take charge of their own biographies. Social class origins may still predict destinations, but via different processes with 'the self' becoming the crucial mediating agent. Another outcome, according to both Beck and Giddens, is a loss of what Giddens calls 'ontological security' (knowing who we are). Individuals are said to seek answers in intimate relationships – pure relationships, unconstrained by any external forces. Individuals remain committed to such relationships only for as long as they find their relationship satisfying. Thus the wider world thrusts people together while their individual paths through this same wider world continuously drive them apart (Beck and Beck-Gernsheim, 1995; Giddens, 1992).

These are features of the latest transformation currently being researched and debated in sociology. Since 1991 the *British Household Panel Survey*, which has been part of the *European Household Panel Survey* since 1995, and was absorbed into and superseded in the UK by the larger longitudinal *Understanding Society* survey in 2009, have been providing data to enable sociology to unravel the connections between macro-trends and micro-social changes.

Seventh, there are further features of the post-industrial age for sociology to address. Some follow the increased international flows of people. These are creating new ethnic relations which are discussed in Chapter 5. Another outcome is the formation of new diaspora (people who identify with an ethnic group or nation whose homeland is elsewhere). The ethnic groups concerned straddle rather than congregate within national borders. Simultaneously, new multi-ethnic milieux are formed. Beck and Beck-Gernsheim (2009) claim that such milieux are experienced as simply normal by many young people today. In London in 2010 nearly 40 per cent of working age residents were born outside the UK (Centre for Economic Performance, 2010). Higher education students find that the student bodies at the universities where they enroll are multi-ethnic and multicultural. Leisure travel, another increasingly common experience for those who can afford it, immerses travellers in multi-ethnic settings at their destinations. The old sociology, in so far as it focused on people who were born and reared, and lived and worked in the same places, among the same people, is unable to cope with these new situations.

Eighth, a further issue is the politics of the new age. Has there simply been a decline of the old social-democratic left and a shift to the right? Or, as Anthony Giddens (1998) claims, has the centre ground become a 'third way' which engages with globalisation, new technologies and environmental challenges, and which seeks to equalise opportunities rather than conditions, and between ethnic groups and men and women as well as social classes? If so, does this new politics amount to an update and revival rather than a retreat from social democracy?

CONCLUSIONS

It will now be evident that sociology has always been embedded as part of the societies that it has studied. This applies to all intellectual life to some extent, but to some segments, particularly the social sciences, more than others. The issues that sociology addresses have always arisen from major changes, transformations, that have been in process or that occurred in the past. As pointed out in Chapter 1, this does not mean that all sociologists research and write about industrialisation, social democracy and/or post-industrialism. Most have more specific interests in education, crime, the family or whatever. Nevertheless, what makes their work sociological is an awareness that the characteristics of education and all other specific parts of a society are somehow products or manifestations of the wider context.

It will also be fully evident that different groups within a society have been and continue to be affected in different ways by all the transformations discussed above and in Chapter 2, and it is also the case that the momentum behind the transformations has come from particular sections of the populations. Thus, alongside transformations, sociology's twin core interest has always been in social divisions.

4. Divisions: social class

INTRODUCTION

The transformations in Chapters 2 and 3 were not the unaided work of impersonal forces of history. Durkheim may have believed that the progressive division of labour had made industrialisation both possible and necessary, but Weber, his contemporary, realised that this transformation had needed motivated people to push history forward. Weber thought that Protestant religion had been the spark. Comte's view had been that a new scientific outlook on life and nature was responsible. Marx, followed by Weber in this respect, believed that a particular social group, in Marx's case the bourgeoisie, had led the changes. They had realised that harnessing new technologies to the factory system and wage labour would enable them to accumulate wealth as never before. They may not, indeed could not, have been aware of how their efforts, collectively, would transform society, but it was their efforts that were responsible rather than just historical destiny. Marx also realised that the development of industrial capitalism was having different effects among different sections of the population. The bourgeoisie were growing richer. Workers, Marx believed, would continue to be paid mere subsistence wages and were being subjected to greater alienation than their peasant predecessors.

Present-day sociologists are agreed that social changes, not least major transformations, are usually the work of particular groups or coalitions who have particular aims and interests, and that the consequences of change are always filtered by the prevailing social divisions. So the core issues in sociology have always been about social transformations, social divisions and their interrelationships.

Class was the original social division on sociology's agenda. Before differences among people can become issues for sociology the differences must be seen as socially constructed rather than inevitable expressions of nature. This was manifestly true of the division and relationship between capitalist employers and wage labourers. This relationship was so recent that it could not have been an inevitable outcome of God or nature making some high and others lowly. Thus class became a major issue during the birth of sociology and has remained so ever since.

Other divisions have been added to sociology's mainstream agenda only since 1945. Race was previously treated as a scientific category. Nothing is ever 100 per cent agreed, especially in science, but the prevailing view had been that humanity was divided into different races, each with its own capabilities and limitations. This is why social anthropology, at that time the study of allegedly simple societies (by Europeans and North Americans), was allied to general anthropology, the study of humanity's physical characteristics. Sociologists focused on modern societies, and adopted the view of 'simpler' societies as represented in the work of social anthropologists. Matters changed only after the Second World War and the Holocaust. The United Nations appointed a commission to interrogate racial theories. Its conclusion was that there is a single human race, and that physical differences between human groups have no necessary psychological or social implications. By this time colonial peoples were demanding freedom and independence, and a civil rights movement was mobilising in the USA. Henceforth in sociology all political, economic and social differences between people of what had been called different races have been treated as requiring a sociological explanation. Thus race moved from anthropology onto sociology's agenda.

Before long gender became another mainstream sociological issue. Until the 1960s the orthodox view was that the differences between the lives of men and women were outcomes of their different biological natures. This appeared confirmed after the feminist movements of the late-nineteenth and early-twentieth centuries secured equal political and legal rights for women. However, by the end of the 1960s a second-wave feminist movement was in full swing. Sociologists distinguished between *sex differences* (the biological differences between males and females) and *gender differences* (everything that is socially constructed on the basis of sex differences). Subsequently a domain assumption (working hypothesis) in mainstream sociology has been that any differences between men's and women's positions in politics, employment and family roles, and their leisure lives, require a sociological explanation.

Since the 1960s class, race/ethnicity (see Chapter 5) and gender have been the main divisions studied by sociology, but by the end of the twentieth century additional divisions – by age, sexuality and ability/disability – were being pressed onto the agenda. Ageing is like sex differences – simply given by nature – but this does not apply to matters such as the ages when young people are able to obtain adult jobs or claim adult welfare rights, or the ages at which people are allowed or obliged to retire from employment on full pensions. Issues like age are taken-up by sociology when customary arrangements change and therefore cease to appear inevitable, and/or when enough people begin to argue that the relevant practices could and should be different.

Sociology is interested in whether heterosexuality and homosexuality are inbred or socially learnt preferences, but more so in how and why people of different sexualities may be treated differently, and the outcomes in the rest of their lives. Sociology adopted this issue following gay liberation movements challenging *hetero-normativity* (treating heterosexuality alone as normal) then demanding that gays, lesbians and bi-sexuals be treated as simply different rather than perverted, and accorded the same respect as heterosexuals.

Disability entered sociology's agenda in much the same way. Clearly, there are physical differences between blind and sighted people, the deaf and the hearing, the limbless and the full-bodied. These differences become problems for sociology when it is argued that being blind or confined to a wheelchair is a social handicap only for as long as social institutions are designed for the majority, that is, for people who are sighted and who can move independently. Some argue that most, if not all jobs, would be within the capabilities of most differently abled people if the jobs were redesigned. The same argument can be posed in relation to opportunities in education and politics. The obstacles are then seen to be as much social and physical.

Most of us are not only affected by, but at some points in our lives are likely to feel affected by class, gender and age divisions. For others, the divisions that matter most are by race/ethnicity, sexuality or ability/ disability. With all these divisions, sociology is interested in their role in producing, and then in how the different groups have been affected differently by, the social transformations in Chapters 2 and 3.

The last chapter noted the difficulty in selecting a label for the outcome of the latest social transformation. The choice of post-industrial was from a number of options. It is always easiest to outline the main features of an era that has become history. The origins of social democracy and the changes that it achieved are more easily listed now that the era seems to have ended. A perpetual problem for sociology in a changing world is that its stock of concepts and explanations may look out-of-date. Karl Marx's ideas were formed during the development of industrial capitalism almost 200 years ago. Capitalism as analysed by Marx does not map perfectly onto the present-day economy, and the same applies to all earlier sociology whether about class, race or gender. We always have to decide whether to try to develop and build on earlier work, or jettison it and start afresh. We misuse and fail to derive potential benefits from earlier conceptualisations when we treat them as hypotheses to test, then probably reject them. They are likely to prove useful aids in examining a different present day. So the starting point in addressing class (and gender and race) divisions must be to appraise our theoretical heritage.

KARL MARX: RELATIONSHIPS TO THE MEANS OF PRODUCTION

Marx treated the bourgeoisie and proletariat as the two great classes of capitalism. This was not mainly on grounds of size. It was partly because other classes (mainly peasants and the self-employed) were expected to be absorbed into one of the two great classes. However, the bourgeoisie and proletariat were considered great mainly on account of their historical missions. The bourgeoisie was formed from artisans and traders who realised that with modern technologies, water then steam power, the factory system and wage labour, they could develop their businesses to a previously unimaginable extent. Part of the bourgeoisie's revolutionary role was spreading new relationships of production. They hired 'free' wage labour. Workers were free to leave an employer except that they needed employment in order to secure livelihoods. Employers needed to hire, pay and retain only the numbers required at any time. Workers were made responsible for reproducing their own labour power from day-to-day (feeding, resting and recuperating) and from generation to generation (procreating and rearing future workers). Marx was convinced that in creating this proletariat the bourgeoisie were their own grave diggers. He believed that there was bound to be perpetual conflict over hours of work, the pace of work, conditions at work and rates of pay. Such conflicts were all about surplus value – how much would be created and how it should be distributed. Marx was convinced that a time would come when the proletariat realised that they could dispense with the bourgeoisie, take control over the means of production, create a society in which property was owned communally, where everyone's needs could be met, where there would be no basis for conflict, where people could collectively control their lives, and thus alienation would end.

Present-day Marxists believe very little of this just as present-day Christians are unlikely to treat the Bible as literal truth. Marx's ideas have been revised constantly by supporters, beginning even before his demise. Lenin developed Marx's thinking into Marxism-Leninism. Outside Communist countries Marxists needed to develop their theory, first of all to explain the absence of the revolution that Marx had envisaged. They also recognised that other classes were not disappearing. The petit bourgeoisie, the self-employed, amount to around 15 per cent of the labour forces in most capitalist countries today. Also, all these countries have experienced an expansion of their middle classes who are neither part of the bourgeoisie nor proletarians.

Marxists have offered various explanations for the absence of a revolution: rising living standards producing contented workers, the cultural industries providing entertainment which makes the masses feel happy; sexual repression in the family which trains workers to curb their instincts and submit to authority; and control by ideological apparatuses (education, mass media and religion). An outcome can be that capitalism is experienced as hegemonic – the way things are and have to be, rather like the geographical terrain and the weather.

Present-day Marxists do not necessarily expect the proletariat to develop a revolutionary consciousness even in the long run. They may well have concluded that capitalism could endure indefinitely. Their contention, and the sense in which they remain true to Marx, lies in insisting that their theory offers the best explanations of all the above. They insist that classes, defined by their relationships to the means of production, and the conflicts of interest between them, are still the main drivers of historical change. The advent of social democracy is seen as an outcome of the working-classes mobilising, becoming a political force, and bringing about the relevant changes. The shift into a post-industrial age, the resurgence of neo-liberal economics and all that has followed, is explained in terms of a change, to the detriment of the working class, in the balance of class forces. It is said that capital has escaped from the control of national governments, exposed workers in different countries to competition between one another, and introduced new technologies which enable surplus value to be created and extracted in greater quantities than ever before. The labour internationalism that would empower resistance is still awaited.

Marxists do not claim that the classes that exist today are exactly those that Marx himself identified, but they insist that Marx was right in arguing that classes are formed by their relationships to the means of production. Erik Olin Wright (2000), an American sociologist, claims to apply this Marxist formula in identifying the following classes:

- Capitalists, the grand bourgeoisie of wealthy shareholders whose lifestyles and life chances depend on capital accumulation and returns.
- A petit bourgeoisie: the self-employed with and without employees.
- Managers, who are in the contradictory situation of being salaried yet performing functions of capital, including the control of other workers.
- Professionals, highly qualified experts who, like managers, receive a share of surplus value on account of their importance to their employers.

- Workers, among whom those with supervisory responsibilities, and the more highly skilled, can be distinguished from the pure proletariat who sell simply their labour power.

Each of these classes is said to be formed and sustained through its relationships with other classes, and the pivotal relationship, generating all the other relationships, is said to be that between employers and workers. Each class is believed to have its own interests, and the Marxist contention is that the dynamic relationships between these classes either keep the system stable or drive history forward.

Allocating individuals to classes in Wright's (2000) scheme is accomplished by asking survey respondents whether they wholly or partly own the businesses where they work, if so whether they employ anyone else, then the size of the business. Non-owners are separated into classes according to whether they have management or supervisory responsibilities, and whether they have skills (certified by educational qualifications) that are used in their jobs. 'No' to all these questions leaves members of a pure proletariat.

The Wright scheme is rarely used in survey research. There are several reasons for this. First, all other measurements of class place people according to their occupations. So all solicitors are placed in the same class, all waiters likewise and so on. Wright has always treated job and occupational titles sceptically. He has been especially sceptical of the liberal use of 'manager'. So his scheme requires people to be asked a series of questions about their own jobs, which is less straightforward than simply obtaining their occupations. Second, the Wright procedures lead to some placements that look 'odd'. For example, people in well-paid jobs in financial services may be placed in the proletariat because they manage no one and have no qualifications that are relevant to their jobs. Skilled workers are liable to be removed from the proletariat because they hold intermediate vocational qualifications despite this 'aristocracy of labour' having been a vanguard in organised labour movements. Third, critics ask whether the scheme is truly Marxist. Should qualifications play any role in a genuinely Marxist class scheme? Finally, very similar classes are identified in other class schemes, and the findings from the relevant research can easily be given a Marxist interpretation, if desired.

MAX WEBER: MARKETS, EXCLUSION AND CLOSURE

Weber's manuscripts that have been published after his death includes an essay (apparently unfinished) on 'class, status and party' (see Gerth and

Mills, 1946). In it Weber states that classes are products of markets, implying that class will be a major form of stratification only in societies where markets play a major role, that is, in modern capitalist societies. This is consistent with Weber's other writings. Status groups, in Weber's view, were an alternative or complementary way in which people could be stratified. Status groups were said to be distinguished by the degrees of honour (prestige) attached to their styles of life. Weber's examples of status groups included castes in India and the *junkers*, Prussia's land owning aristocracy. Weber clearly regarded class stratification, or at least its prominence, as a modern phenomenon.

The conceptual distinction between class and status is clear enough, and some sociologists have attempted to distinguish classes from status groups within modern societies, though it is not clear that the status associated with a lifestyle today can be independent of the class positions of the actors. The different degrees of 'honour' associated with going to the opera and attending football matches are probably wholly explicable in terms of the social composition of the audiences and crowds. Sociologists have sometimes treated status as an attribute of occupations, and as a satisfactory indicator of their class positions (though neither Marxist nor Weberian sociologists accept occupational status as a satisfactory indicator of class). Nevertheless, this practice acknowledges the close correspondence between class and status today.

However, there are serious differences between Marx's and Weber's explanations of class formation. Weber lived a generation after Marx, and can be regarded as debating with Marx, or the Marxism of his own lifetime, and more often qualifying Marx rather than offering a diametrically opposed analysis. Weber believed that classes had become prominent only along with the growth in the importance of markets in the modern world. Marx regarded all societies where there had been a separate group who owned the means of production as class societies, though the character of the classes changed along with the forces and details of the relationships of production. The related Marx-Weber disagreement lies in Marx identifying 'relationships of production' as the root source of class divisions whereas for Weber classes arose in market places. A basic class division, in Weber's view, was between those who hired and those who sold their labour – the same class schism that Marx identified. However, Weber believed that that there could be different classes of workers defined by the kinds of labour that they could offer – their levels and types of skills. Groups of workers could organise in trade unions or professional associations and seek to close entry to their positions, that is, to exclude outsiders. Exclusion (of those below) and usurpation (attempting to break into higher levels of employment) were processes that split workforces into classes. Thus Weberian sociologists have always been comfortable in identifying different classes of workers, whereas Marxists have seen only 'ambiguous' or 'contradictory' class locations, like those of managers, and have regarded all divisions among workers as products of the bourgeoisie's divide and rule tactics.

Weber was deeply interested in politics, and 'parties' (in his meaning) were groups mobilised to seek power. Weber believed that the pursuit and defence of power could be ends in themselves rather than means to promote or protect the interests of a particular class or status group. He believed that successful 'parties' would typically be coalitions of classes (or class factions) and maybe status groups rather than based squarely on any one of these. Marxists are unlikely to dissent from any of this except to stress the huge advantages of having the support of capital.

Although they start by defining class differently, and have different ideas on exactly how classes are formed, present-day Marxist and Weberian sociologists come to very similar conclusions about the principal classes in contemporary societies. Weberians (for example Goldthorpe et al., 1980), who treat Weber himself as qualifying or adding to Marxism, identify the following classes:

- An upper class of the extremely wealthy.
- A petit bourgeoisie: the self-employed, with and without employees.
- A service class or *salariat* of managers and professionals who enjoy trust relationships with their employers.
- A working class, within which employees with supervisory responsibilities may be distinguished, and others can be divided by their levels of skill.
- An intermediate class whose jobs possess some service class features, enough to separate them from the working class (the work environment, and short career ladders, for example), but who are outside the professional and management grades. These include many office and sales staff, technicians and laboratory workers.
- An underclass who are out of the workforce long term and whose main incomes are not from employment. Persons with pensions and other benefits determined by their previous occupations and earnings are not in this group. This class can be regarded as the counterpart of Marx's reserve army of labour that helped to keep wages at a basic subsistence level.

The two largest classes in this scheme are a service class, alternatively called a *salariat* or just middle class, comprising mangers and professional employees, and a working class. These classes are said to be defined by their distinctive market and work situations. The strength of an occupation's 'market situation' can be assessed through the rewards that employees typically receive: earnings of course (and past and future expectations are as important as current incomes), plus any fringe benefits such as pensions, health insurance and use of company cars. 'Work situation' refers to an occupation's typical position in the authority relationships within an organisation. How closely are the employees supervised? Do they command, and are they responsible for the work of other staff? Managers and professionals are said to be distinguished by their superior rewards, and also by the 'trust' relationship with their employers. They are not supervised closely. Official hours of work may often be exceeded. These employees are trusted to use their specialist skills and knowledge in an organisation's interest, and to work as hard and as long as is necessary in order to execute their duties properly.

The working class is in diametrically opposite work and market situations. They are typically paid far less than middle-class employees, and are less likely to be eligible for fringe benefits. There is little trust in the working-class employment relationship. Workers are paid strictly according to the units of time that they work and/or the amounts that they produce. Their attendance and work are closely supervised whether by a human supervisor or by technology. Unlike managers and professionals, they do not have long career ladders that they can ascend, and may well have achieved peak career earnings while in their twenties.

Neither Marxists nor Weberians regard all the classes that they identify as situated linearly above and beneath one another. So the intermediate occupations in a Weberian class scheme are not all below the middle class and above the working class. These are simply different class situations, mainly but not always in the space intermediate between the two largest classes. Similarly the self-employed may be running substantial businesses, earning far more than many professionals and salaried managers. Others may be practising 'survival self-employment' as an alternative to unemployment. They are all grouped together on account of their distinctive work situation – being the boss, responsible only to the market.

Marxists and Weberians both adopt a relational view of class. Classes are seen to be formed through their relationships with one another – employing and being employed, managing and being managed, and (by Weberians) in the labour market through processes of closure and attempted usurpation. The big divide in twentieth century and subsequent sociology has been between these relational, conflict views of class, and those that treat class differences as gradational, expressing value consensus, and fostering integration. The latter, gradational view is not necessarily everyone's normal, everyday, common-sense view of the world, but it is propagated constantly by politicians and the media. Sociologists' arguments are either ignored, or accidently or deliberately misunderstood.

A Weberian class scheme identifying the classes listed above was originally developed by John Goldthorpe for use in a study of social mobility in Britain that was conducted in 1972. In 1998 a version of this scheme was recommended by the social research community and adopted as the official UK class scheme (officially called NS-SEC, which stands for National Statistics – Socio-Economic Classification) and is now used for classifying the population in all UK government statistics. A slightly different version is used for collating comparable data for all European Union countries. Government spokespersons, the media and the general public often treat the scheme as if the classes were all strictly linear. Often they are presumed to represent skill levels, though skill is very difficult to measure objectively, and is not a basis for the placement of occupations. The intermediate classes are not really 'above' but simply different from the working classes, though the intermediate classes are positioned as they are labelled when the scheme is printed and are given digit 3 when coded into computer data-sets while the working classes are 5, 6 and 7. The working classes are not simply below managers and professionals (classes 1 and 2) in being less qualified, less skilled and lower paid, but are subordinated through being 'managed' and, according to Marxists, creating while receiving a far lesser share of surplus value. This is just one example of how difficult it can be for sociology to have its 'way of seeing' adopted more widely.

DURKHEIM, ORGANIC SOLIDARITY AND THE FUNCTIONS OF STRATIFICATION

Durkheim did not write about class, status or stratification. All were subsumed within the 'division of labour' which was supposedly fostering organic solidarity with people bound together by interdependence, and with (unspecified) processes ensuring that role allocation was 'unforced' with everyone performing the roles for which they were best suited. By the mid-twentieth century these ideas had been developed into a functional theory of stratification, stated succinctly by the American sociologists Kingsley Davis and Wilbert Moore in an article first published in 1945. They argued that stratification was necessary to motivate people with scarce but valuable talents to enter positions where they would be most useful to their society, then exercise their talents to the limits of their abilities. The exceptional rewards received by the talented were said to express society's gratitude for their contributions. Thus the entire system of stratification performed an integrative function.

Sociologists who conceptualise stratification in this way prefer not to divide the population into discrete (categorical) classes. They prefer to rank positions (usually occupations) along a continuous scale, portrayed as a ladder up which individuals can attempt to climb, and reach the levels that match their abilities. Occupations are usually ranked according to their prestige. Representative samples of a population are invited to rank occupations according to their prestige. Different sections of a large sample can be presented with different but overlapping lists of occupations, thus enabling large numbers of occupations to be ranked. However, there are thousands of different occupations, and it is impossible to have them all ranked in this way. Also, new occupations are constantly being created and need to be given positions on the class scales without repeating the entire research exercise. The solution to these problems is for scale constructors to discover another indicator which is closely related to prestige. The years spent in education is such a variable. Much larger numbers of occupations can be ranked from information, typically gathered in national censuses, about typical years of education for people practising different occupations. All occupations can then be given precise positions along a continuum and new occupations can be placed in the same way. An alternative procedure is to use 'association' as the indicator of an occupation's prestige level. People are asked to name their closest friends and their occupations, or the occupations of their spouses. The assumption is that people will tend to associate with class equals. Research using both prestige and association as indicators has demonstrated widespread agreement on the ranking of occupations. Thus the inequalities are said to be consensual. However, the fact that people may agree on how occupations are actually ranked does not necessarily mean that they agree on how they ought to be ranked or the scale of the associated inequalities.

From 1911 (when it was first used to analyse the census returns) until 1998, the UK government's official class scheme was actually a prestige scale. Occupations were grouped into one of six classes according to their general social standing. This scheme was known as the Registrar General's Class Scheme and distinguished six groups of occupations:

i.   Higher level managers and professions.
ii.   Lower level managers and professions.
iiia.   Other non-manual.
iiib.   Skilled manual.
iv.   Semi-skilled.
v.   Unskilled.

The UK market research industry continues to use a similar scheme, but labels its classes A, B, Ci, Cii, D and E, and claims that they group together occupations with similar levels of income and households with similar spending patterns. Whichever criteria are used – prestige, income or associates – occupations are usually placed in the same bands or ranked in the same order. The UK government's official class scheme was replaced in 1998 largely on the advice of sociologists whose overwhelming preference was for a relational class scheme.

Sociologists who use gradational measurements of class are not necessarily functionalists, but functionalism necessarily conceptualises class gradationally. Functionalism is sometimes described as a theory that is resurrected every autumn only to be ritually slaughtered for each new cohort of sociology students. The main criticisms of the theory as an explanation of class inequalities are:

- Stratification may create conflict rather than cohesion.
- It can obstruct rather than promote the ascent of the talented and the demotion of dullards.
- The proof is circular and therefore inadmissible. The sole proof of the importance of positions and talents is the prestige and other rewards that they receive, which are then said to prove the importance of the talents and positions.

The functional theory of stratification cannot be pronounced dead because, irrespective of its scientific merits and flaws, it remains a powerful ideology. It is said that managers, lawyers, medical doctors and accountants need to be well-rewarded otherwise those with the requisite abilities would not undertake the initial prolonged training, or continue to keep abreast of knowledge and develop their skills throughout their careers. It is claimed that they would be less likely to put in the hours and effort that their work requires unless they were handsomely rewarded. It is claimed that company directors and bankers need to be paid extremely large salaries, topped up by extremely large bonuses, in order to create career ladders that incentivise those who are already very well-paid to strive for even greater success. It can also be claimed that the theory corresponds to how workers at all levels try to get ahead within the opportunities that are available for them, and how parents encourage their children to do well at school, and experience pride when their children succeed.

American sociologists have been the most likely to use gradational class scales in their research. European sociologists have generally preferred categorical, relational class schemes. The latter, and the underlying theories, are said to be better able to account for:

- Strikes and other forms of industrial conflict.
- Political partisanship; members of different classes tending to vote for different political parties.
- The enormous social class discrepancies in higher education participation rates. In Britain in the early-twenty-first century around 80 per cent of young people from the top managerial and professional groups were progressing into universities against only around 20 per cent from the working class, with only minor differences within the working class by levels of skill. Top universities draw tiny proportions of their students from the poorest families despite protesting that their doors are wide open and that they are making all possible efforts to widen participation.

METHODS OF CLASS ANALYSIS

Nowadays it is very easy for sociologists who wish to do so to employ more than one class scheme or scale and to compare the results. With the exception of Erik Olin Wright's (2000) scheme, where people's actual jobs are allocated to classes, all the schemes and scales group occupations initially into SOCs (Standard Occupational Classification, a government administered instrument). All countries have their own SOCs. They group occupations into similar 'families'. There are around 400 of these families in the current UK SOC, but around double that number in the USA's SOC. However, there is an ISOC (international classification), which is administered by the Geneva-based International Labour Office, into which all national SOCs can be collapsed, thus permitting international comparisons.

Provided an analyst has the necessary software, a computer will allocate SOCs into any of the widely used class schemes and scales. In practice the outcomes are usually very similar. All the instruments group or rank occupations in much the same way. This is to be expected since they all address the same social reality. The differences between the procedures are in the underlying assumptions about how class divisions are formed or how rankings are created, and hence in the likely short- and longer-term outcomes of class inequalities.

Marxists, Weberians and functionalists have fundamental disagreements over how to define class, but their schemes and scales group or rank occupations in very similar ways, and they all adopt occupation as their preferred indicator of class. They also agree that occupation is best used singly. Non-sociologists often ask why not take income, and maybe education and housing into account. All are easily measured but occupation has an overwhelming advantage: the positions of most occupations in the class structure have remained stable over time, and are similar in all modern societies. Education, housing and most other potential class indicators are different in this respect. Attending university has a different significance when this involves less than 10 per cent of young people than when over 50 per cent are enrolling. In the UK, in the 1950s, families who moved into council housing were seen as moving up (from slums). Today a tenancy in social housing is an indicator of disadvantage. Income is an unreliable indicator because it is lifetime income that positions people and entire households. The same annual salary has a different significance when it is the starting grade in a professional career than when it is peak career earnings. The simultaneous use of more than one indicator destroys class divisions and places actors along gradational scales, which is anathema to sociologists who conceptualise class relationally.

Occupation is just an indicator. It is not what class really 'is', namely, positions in the systems of economic production and distribution. That said, people spend many years, and many hours every week throughout all these years, in employment, typically in the same classes of occupations even if they change jobs on several occasions. This makes it likely that their occupations will make an impression on people's consciousness. There is a presumption that people positioned in the same classes of occupations will associate with one another more frequently than with people from other classes if only through working together and living among equals. This makes it possible, though not inevitable, that they will develop class cultures, common lifestyles, perceptions of their interests and hence class-specific political proclivities.

An aim of class analysis is always to investigate the ways and the extent to which occupational aggregates have become social, cultural and political classes. This is likely to be affected by whether they have experienced common types of education, and whether they intermingle with or live apart from other classes. Introducing other variables usually strengthens an analyst's ability to predict outcomes such as voting behaviour and children's attainments in education. Even so, there are still advantages in identifying classes, initially, on the basis of occupations alone. Other indicators either gain their significance from the types of employment to which they typically lead (education) or are typically consequences of people's types of employment (income, and therefore the lifestyles that they can afford).

Most terms in sociology are used in ways that are congruent with their meanings in everyday life, though in sociology the terms are normally used with more precision. We can note here that in all class schemes and scales people are placed independently of their own views, if any, on their positions in the class structure. Whether people are class conscious, and if so, the form that this consciousness takes, are issues for sociology to investigate. It is possible for class inequalities to widen while class consciousness diminishes. If so, this is a problem for sociology – something that must be explained. With class and much else, sociology offers a vocabulary than will enable people to better understand their societies and their own positions therein. They should then become more likely, to paraphrase C. Wright Mills (1959), to see how their private troubles can only be properly addressed by recognising that they are really widely shared public issues.

An issue to which contemporary sociology has no agreed answer concerns the unit to classify – the individual or the family-household – and if the latter, whose occupations to take into account. Conventional practice used to be to classify households on the basis of a (usually male) head of household's occupation. As two or more earner families have become increasingly common, this conventional practice has grown outdated. However, a problem in taking all earners' occupations into account, for sociologists who adopt a relational view of class, is that doing so obliterates class divisions and produces a gradational scale. If the household is to be classified, the normal practice is still to use the occupation of a main earner.

The alternative is to classify individuals, and this has become the new conventional practice in sociology. It can be justified by the increased levels of labour market participation by women, later ages of first marriages, and higher rates of separation and divorce, making both sexes' life chances dependent mainly on their own qualifications and occupations. However, this results, for example, in all women in lower level non-manual jobs being placed in the same intermediate class irrespective of whether their partners are managers or accountants, or caretakers or security guards. The crucial fact of this matter is that in present-day society none of the alternatives looks appropriate for all cases. A compromise is to use the household when household behaviour and outcomes are being examined (standards of living and the educational attainments of children, for example), and to classify individuals when their personal behaviour and attitudes (such as voting intentions) are being examined.

CLASS IN POST-INDUSTRIAL SOCIETY

All sociology's class schemes and scales are able to cope with change. Indeed, these instruments are essential if we are to understand the sources and wider social outcomes of economic changes: those that followed the Second World War, and then the later shift into a post-industrial age. However, we (in sociology) have a problem with our limited, widely understood vocabulary. We can refer to upper, middle and working classes, sometimes using prefixes so as to distinguish upper-middle from lower-middle and so on, but the very use of these terms may appear to position the thinking in the past, when this vocabulary was first widely used. The terminology may appear to be rooted in the earlier age when a manual working class was the largest class, organised in trade unions which supported political parties of the left which sought to extend state control if not outright ownership of the economy and to develop welfare states. These were the movements that built the West's social democracies. The middle classes, in fact everyone who felt threatened rather than represented by working-class power, tended to support parties of the right.

In post-industrial societies both the working and middle classes are different than formerly, and they do not differ from one another in exactly the same ways as in the past. In industrial enterprises there used to be a clear distinction between staff and works, salaried versus hourly paid, who had different work schedules, eligibility for fringe benefits, and quite likely separate toilets and canteens. Subsequently new technologies have entered offices, and simultaneously have removed most of the grime and physical effort from 'manual' occupations. The issues for class analysis in present-day sociology arise from changes such as this. What are the causes and what are the social, cultural and political consequences?

In the UK the proportion of employees who are in trade unions is now highest in the management and professional grades. The image of trade unionism as a working-class movement is out-of-date. The change is due to the highly unionised public sector employing large numbers in the management and professional grades in central and local government, education and health services. An outcome is that trade unionism has ceased to be a distinctively working-class movement.

The relationship between class and voting behaviour has weakened. Table 4.1 presents voting intentions just prior to the 2010 UK general election. This table uses the class scheme still favoured by market researchers. The ABs are managers and professional employees, C1s are other non-manuals, C2s are skilled manual workers and DEs are the rest. The self-employed are placed according to their occupations. This same class scheme has been used in studies of voting behaviour since the 1960s. At that time at least three-quarters of the ABs could be relied on to vote Conservative whereas in 2010 just 39 per cent did so, and there was almost as much Conservative support among the C2s (37 per cent). Labour used to command at least two-thirds of working-class votes whereas in 2010 it was supported by only 29 per cent of the C2s and 40 per cent of the DEs. This does not necessarily mean that class divisions have weakened. This could be the explanation. Alternatively it could be that politics, specifically

Table 4.1   Class and voting intentions, 2010 UK general election (in percentages)

	AB	C1	C2	DE
Conservative	39	39	37	31
Labour	26	28	29	40
Liberal Democrat	29	24	22	17
Other	7	9	12	12

Notes: AB – managers and professional employees; C1 – other non-manuals; C2 – skilled manual workers; DE – the rest. Self-employed are placed according to their occupations.

Source: MORI.

the main political parties, have changed. The latter is the most likely explanation since the relationship between children's social class background and their attainments in education remains as strong as ever. Class continues to predict levels of sports participation and much else just as powerfully as ever. The class structure has changed, but change does not necessarily mean weakened.

Employment has changed during the shift into a post-industrial age, with inevitable implications for the character of different classes, and the differences and relationships between them.

- There is now a large, service sector-based proletariat that is employed, for example, in supermarkets, retail parks, hospitality, call centres, small shops, care homes, nurseries, cleaning and security businesses, and sometimes as gardeners and nannies who work in private homes. Few are in trade unions. Much of this employment is part-time. Low pay is the norm. Many of the employees are young. Students often take the part-time jobs. Another expanding group are older workers who have been displaced (sometimes having been retired early) from their main career occupations. For others, often females, these are their main lifetime occupations. Recent immigrants (legal or otherwise) are another group who are over-represented within this service sector-based proletariat.
- A working-class aristocracy, as it may now be described, though not necessarily skilled in traditional senses, is employed in the public sector and large private sector businesses such as oil refineries, car plants and in transport. These employees are mostly in trade unions. Most of the jobs are full-time, generally better paid, and more secure than the service sector proletariat's employment. This

'traditional', mainly male, working class is much smaller today than in the past.

- In post-industrial societies it has become common for at least 50 per cent of all young people to undertake tertiary/higher education. The qualifications earned are likely to be required for entry to any job in offices performing clerical and data processing duties, in sales occupations and in laboratories. These occupations have become the normal starting jobs for university graduates. In the early-twentieth century the junior non-manual grades were normal starting-points for persons who trained to become solicitors, accountants and other professionals, and from which many ascended to become managers. At that time it was realistic to treat all non-manual employees as part of a layered but unitary middle class. By the mid-twentieth century lower level office work was largely feminised, and these grades were more clearly apart from the management and professional occupations into which young people were recruited directly from expanded systems of higher education. Today, following a further expansion of higher education, the middle class is experiencing further restructuring. Higher education itself is now more clearly stratified. Graduates from 'top' universities enter directly into professional and management trainee posts. Other graduates enter intermediate level jobs in offices, sales work and laboratories from which they are unlikely to advance beyond the junior management and professional levels.
- Some professions benefit in terms of the rewards that they can command from shortages of the relevant skills, not because the skills are exceptionally difficult to learn or practise, but because opportunities to acquire the skills and gain relevant experience are restricted. This applies in medicine, law, accountancy, the engineering professions and in City occupations (but not retail banking). Entry is difficult for anyone who has not graduated from a 'top' university.
- Employees who work for and have direct responsibility for deploying capital (company directors, investment bankers and fund managers, for example) are exceptionally rewarded. These employees can become seriously rich, thereby aligning their own interests with those of the (global) capitalist class.

Class analysis is as vital as ever. Otherwise we are unable to understand what is happening in the world of work, and how this is changing education and so many other aspects of the lives of people in all social classes.

CONCLUSIONS

A point to note is that Marxist and Weberian concepts – relationships to the means of production, market situations, closure and exclusion – are capable of handling all the processes creating older and newer class formations and divisions. Functionalism may well explain differences in levels of rewards and career progression within each 'class' of employment, but looks far less plausible when confronted by the sheer scale of the differences in rewards between the various classes.

These original sociological approaches to class analysis have proved impressively serviceable. They have proved applicable in the early decades of industrialism, during the social-democratic era, and now in post-industrial times. Moreover, they identify classes that have instigated and shaped these transformations, and have distinguished how different sections of the populations of modern societies have been affected. These theories are not sets of hypotheses to test. Rather, they are sometimes alternative but at other times complementary and compatible 'ways of seeing', what are sometimes called 'paradigms' (see Chapter 7). They survive for as long as they can accommodate new class divisions and processes of class formation, and up to the present, collectively, they have met all challenges.

5.   Gender, race and other divisions

GENDER

Introduction

Second-wave feminism forced gender onto sociology's research agenda and syllabuses during the 1960s. The young women who became part of this feminist movement were from the post-war post-scarcity generation who wanted more freedom to live their lives as they saw fit. Previously the orthodox view was that males and females were metaphorically from Mars and Venus, and had evolved so that men were more suited to hunting (earning livelihoods for their families), warfare (protecting their families) and ruling (originally because men were the physically stronger). Females, in contrast, were designed for breeding, naturally suited to nurturing children and driven by a mothering instinct. As such, women needed male protectors whose loyalty they could retain by providing sexual gratification, producing heirs and maintaining warm, caring havens to which men could return from the harsher outside world. These beliefs underpinned the ideal bourgeois family. It was described as bourgeois because the ideal was believed to have its origins within the bourgeoisie (the propertied middle class), and it was only within this class that reality could approximate to the ideal.

First-wave feminism had won formal legal and political equalities in the early-twentieth century. Women had won the vote, the right to be elected to public offices, to own property irrespective of marital status and to divorce on the same grounds as men. However, the freedom to discriminate had been left intact. Employers could and did specify which jobs were for men and which were for women. Employers were free, if they wished, as many did, to offer different rates of pay to men and women who did exactly the same jobs. It was perfectly legal to discriminate in favour of men in promotion decisions. In education boys and girls could be and were offered different male and female subjects. Second-wave feminists protested that all this was blatantly unfair, and insisted that the relevant attitudes and practices should be changed. Discrimination on the grounds of sex is now illegal in employment, education and most public services, and likewise sexual harassment. Feminism has also been successful in making domestic violence a public issue. The world's first women's refuge was opened by Erin Pizzey in Chiswick (London) in 1971. Formerly domestic violence against women had rarely been checked because the police refused to treat domestic incidents as crimes. Campaigns for women's rights forced changes in police practices, and since 1990 in the UK domestic violence units with specially trained officers have been established in most police forces. The courts of law formerly refused to accept that rape could occur within marriage. In the USA South Dakota became the first state to make spousal rape a crime in 1975: it is now illegal in 50 states. In the UK it was not until 1991 that the House of Lords ruled that the marital rights exemption was a common law fiction, and successful prosecutions for marital rape became possible.

Since the rise of second-wave feminism the orthodox view in sociology, a domain assumption, has been that all differences in the social roles of men and women are socially constructed gender differences, capable of being reconstructed. Anyone refusing to accept this as axiomatic has been liable to dismissal as an unreconstructed male chauvinist (if a man) or in urgent need of enlightenment (if female). We need to bear in mind throughout that domain assumptions are just assumptions, as yet unproven, and in this case probably incapable of being proven. Domain assumptions of some type underlie all sociological enquiry and analysis, and can remain assumptions for as long, but only as long, as they are plausible in the face of the available (though less than conclusive) evidence.

Liberal Reform

Between the 1960s and 1980s all Western countries made it illegal to have different rates of pay for men and women who were doing the same jobs. European law (enforced by the courts in all member countries) has subsequently prescribed equal pay for work of equal value (although it is difficult, arguably impossible, to measure value objectively). National and European legislation also proscribes discrimination in hiring, access to training and promotion, to educational programmes, and to virtually all publicly available services. The UK passed the Equal Pay Act in 1970 and the Equal Opportunities Act in 1975. At that time similar measures were outlawing racial discrimination. Additional liberalising reforms were giving women, irrespective of marital status, access to contraception and abortion (in most Western countries), and introducing equal treatment for men and women in tax and benefit regimes, once again irrespective of marital status. Affordable and accessible childcare has been a further demand (so far only partly met in many countries). These measures began to be introduced and implemented in the age of social democracy. Thomas H. Marshall (1963), a UK sociologist, conceptualised these changes as extending citizenship. People had already won civic citizenship (the right to the protection of the law and courts) and political citizenship (the right to vote). Citizenship was being extended into social domains giving people rights to education, health care, income maintenance, the right to employment and so on. Eradicating sex discrimination meant making women first class, full citizens, instead of allowing them to be treated as second class, with some rights accessed only via their male partners.

The liberal position on gender is that changing discriminatory laws and outlawing discriminatory practices should be sufficient because afterwards people will behave equitably. Equalising opportunities and treatment is seen as a win-win reform. No one loses. Society is able to benefit fully from both sexes' talents which should be in everyone's interest: an optimal, unforced outcome of the division of labour. It can be argued that men have an interest in, and as much to gain as women from gender equity. A new 'men's studies' in sociology has pointed out that men can feel as constrained by the conventional male role as women feel when expected to be submissive and to prioritise motherhood and caring. Many boys have suffered from the expectation that they should enjoy rough competitive sports. Why should those so inclined feel inhibited in taking-up nursing and other caring professions? Given gender equality in access to all types of education and employment, there should be no disadvantage overall if men were as likely to spend periods as househusbands as women as housewives.

The criticism of the liberal position is that the changes that have resulted have been too modest and too slow: *Slow Motion* is the title of Lynne Segal's (2007) repeatedly reissued book. In the UK, as in all other Western countries, the gap between male and female earnings has narrowed but it has not been eliminated. Men are doing more housework and child-care, but women still do far more than men. Women have been breaking through glass ceilings. There are more women managers and company directors, and more women are being elected to public bodies, but we remain a long way from gender parity. There have been several responses to this situation:

- Be patient; this type of change unfolds over generations.
- Equitable treatment does not have to lead to identical outcomes – identical proportions of men and women taking all educational courses and in all jobs. Once discrimination has been removed, different outcomes may reflect the different wishes and maybe the different natures of men and women.

- The legislation needs to be strengthened: for example, by compulsory audits which force businesses to justify inequalities among their employees, by requiring equal representation of men and women on company boards, on all elected bodies and on appointed public bodies.
- There are additional barriers to gender equity that need to be removed.

Marxist-feminism

The same theoretical positions reappear in debates in sociology about all the main divisions – class, gender and race. Some believe that ending unnecessary discrimination will lead to a division of labour in which neither sex feels forced into roles for which they are unsuited. Marxists (this theory was extremely influential in Western sociology between the 1960s and 1980s) counter-argue that the oppression of women (like divisions among workers) is another manifestation of capitalist exploitation and will end only with the advent of socialism.

Friedrich Engels, Marx's collaborator and patron, wrote the first Marxist account of the family. He argued that families were first formed alongside the creation of private property and a separate class of owners who appropriated surplus value. This was when families became necessary so that property could be passed on to heirs. For this to happen women had to become the sexual property of their husbands to whom their sexual relationships were confined. Formerly there was supposed to have been an age of primitive communism and its counterpart of sexual communism where children belonged to the entire community. Social anthropologists have never encountered such societies. Engels' history was entirely speculative. Nevertheless, there was an attempt to implement this theory in some of the early socialist kibbutzim in Palestine/Israel where all productive assets were owned communally and children belonged to the kibbutz. This experiment did not work and eventually family relationships, residences and parent-child relationships were permitted then became the norm.

However, Marxists have identified additional ways in which the capitalist class benefits from the oppression of women. The reproduction of labour power is made the responsibility of women. 'Reproduction' here means the procreation and rearing of children (reproduction from generation to generation) and also reproduction from day-to-day by facilitating the rest and recuperation of male workers. All this essential reproductive labour is undertaken without payment by employers. Women and children are supported from supposedly family wages earned by husbands and fathers. The value of women's unpaid work (estimated by what it would cost to purchase the relevant services on the market) is enormous, yet completely ignored in national accounts from which the gross domestic product (GNP) and standards of living are calculated. Only work for employers where a good or service can be marketed, thereby in principle enabling surplus value to be extracted, is included in 'capitalist' national accounts. Marxists regard this as another capitalist distortion. Women's skills and efforts are systematically devalued. The normal family arrangement enables women who are employed to be hired on submale rates of pay. Women are deemed secondary earners. Tacit skills that they bring into workplaces – the ability to cook, clean and generally care for other employees and customers – are taken-for-granted and the work is likely to be classified as non-skilled. The working classes as a whole, but working-class women in particular, are seen as having an interest in the overthrow of capitalism. The proposed route is an alliance of socialists and (some) feminists – the core of a so-called progressive rainbow coalition that might succeed where the unaided male working class has failed.

The plausibility of this thinking faded during the 1980s. The lives of women in the existing socialist states looked less liberated the better they were known. It is true that Soviet women were used extensively in what in the West have been considered male occupations – medical doctors (not a well-paid occupation in the Soviet bloc), construction trades and road clearing, and also as soldiers (during the Second World War Germany and her allies found themselves fighting against soldiers in skirts). However, men occupied nearly all the power positions as plant directors and members of the *politburo* (the Soviet equivalent of a government cabinet). Also, Soviet women were not relieved of the double-shift – they were still expected to perform nearly all housework and take responsibility for childcare. Soviet man proved to be just as conventionally masculine as Western man.

Marxist-feminism also lost its appeal during the transition to a post-industrial age, in which the proposed overthrow of capitalism began to look more distant than ever. Communism collapsed, capitalism became a truly global system and the West's main parties of the left abandoned socialist aims. This was the context in which, for most Western feminists, the enemy became not capitalism but patriarchy.

Patriarchy

This is a system of male power, the rule of women by men. Families, businesses, governments and entire societies may be patriarchal. It is claimed that patriarchy preceded and has continued under not only capitalism but throughout the entire modern era. Modernisation is seen as a project that was led by and for men. The great names in history whatever the field – explorers, traders, empire builders, scientists, manufacturers, financiers, military leaders and even sociologists – are nearly all men's names. In creating modern institutions it is said that males (patriarchs) separated public and private realms. The public realm was masculine, created by men for men, and required masculine qualities. Women were confined to the private realm of home, appearing in the public realm mainly as assets (trophies) of their menfolk.

Patriarchy's roots in history could lie in men being the physically stronger sex along with the demands of childbearing and child rearing making women dependent on male providers and protectors. However, it is claimed that modernity has given women the means to liberate themselves. The rule of law and the monopolisation of force by states has neutralised males' superior physical strength. Access to contraception and abortion enable women to control their fertility. Schools, kindergartens and nurseries plus domestic technology make it unnecessary for housework and child rearing to be full-time occupations. The post-industrial economy has eliminated many jobs that required masculine skills. Service sector occupations are more likely to require traditionally feminine qualities, especially occupations involving customer care. However, for women to escape from patriarchy it is argued that the first step must be for women to redefine themselves.

The French existentialist and writer, Simone de Beauvoir (1972), was the first to note explicitly how women had been subjected to 'othering'. This occurs when one group is defined by, and in the interests of, another group. The contention here is that femininity has been constructed by men, in men's interests. Women are defined as naturally submissive, caring and unsuited to heavy responsibilities. Women therefore need men to shelter and guide them through life. This is the sense in which Simone de Beauvoir contended that women were the 'second sex' – through being defined by, in this sense created by, and typically internalising the identities imposed by men. We shall see later that this 'othering' concept has subsequently been put to wider use in sociology.

The implication of this analysis is that the fundamental step in challenging and overthrowing patriarchy must be for women to make themselves independent of men. This will mean achieving economic independence (earning their own livings), gaining full citizenship and welfare rights rather than being treated as dependents, controlling their own fertility and making themselves emotionally and socially independent – hence the case for political lesbianism. Women, it is said, must first of all redefine themselves, understand how they have been oppressed, how this has shaped their own identities and having done so they may re-engage with men on equal terms. A sociology that facilitates this is described as 'emancipatory'.

An offshoot from this case for women developing their own standpoint has been a searing critique of 'malestream' sociology. The 'founding fathers' were all men. It is claimed that sociology has consistently adopted a male view of the world which cannot be rectified by simply tacking-on women to syllabuses on crime, education, work and so on. Standpoint feminism (see Smith, 1990) seeks to rework all knowledge from the woman's perspective.

This opens a series of questions that are taken-up in later chapters of this book. Can there be an objective standpoint? Can any woman speak for all women irrespective of class and race? Can any person claim to see society as would anyone except himself or herself? Some claim that as victims women occupy a privileged position for viewing and understanding the operation of patriarchy. There is a parallel claim about the working class having the best understanding of capitalism. These claims are tenuous. Victims will be able to speak only as victims and maybe for other victims. The formation of different standpoints has threatened sociology with chaos.

Gender in Post-industrial Society

The historical shift into a post-industrial age has changed gender roles and divisions, and the character of the gender issue in sociology. Feminism has lost its former traction. Young women are no longer joining women's caucuses. Maybe they are less interested in winning yet more freedoms than in using the opportunities that they now possess, some won by feminism, others delivered by history. Conditions are very different today than in the 1960s when second-wave feminism gained momentum.

- The contraceptive pill, marketed since 1961, took longer to be taken-up, but its use is now normal among young single women. Combined with access to abortion, this has given women effective control over their own fertility. The outcomes include typical ages of first births rising into late-20s and 30s. These women can become established in occupational careers before becoming mothers. They usually take maternity leave instead of career breaks, and can build scarcely interrupted employment careers.
- Girls now out-perform boys at all levels in education – in primary then secondary schools, and young women are now the majority of undergraduates in higher education in all Western (and many other) countries. Previously girls typically did better than boys in

primary school, but thereafter the males pulled ahead. There are still differences in the subjects that males and females study. Males predominate in engineering and women in arts and languages, but overall young women enter the labour market better-qualified than young men.

- In terms of employment opportunities, the shift into a post-industrial age has been woman-friendly. Heavy industrial jobs performed mainly by men have been lost. There are more non-manual jobs, always considered more suitable for women, in public administration, education and health services, banking and retailing.
- The proportion of women who are employed in management and professional occupations has risen to the same level as among men. As lower level office jobs have been lost to technology, better-qualified young women have been moving up into the professional and management grades.
- Women have been breaking through former glass ceilings. The UK had its first female Prime Minister, Margaret Thatcher, between 1979 and 1990. Since 2005 the USA's Secretaries of State have been women – Condoleezza Rice followed by Hillary Rodham Clinton. Women are still under-represented in power positions, but they are better represented than in the past in politics and company boardrooms.
- Young women have widened their repertoires when at leisure. They are now as likely as young men to play indoor sports (which is where most sport is played today).
- Although men still consume more alcohol, women have been closing the gap.

As noted above, some say that these changes have not gone far enough. This raises the question of 'Not far enough for whom?' 'Not far enough' may be a valid feminist observation about society in general, but this is not the same as women complaining that their personal opportunities are restricted because of their sex. Catherine Hakim (2004) argues that women tend to have different aspirations than men, and that there are differences among women. A few still aspire to be full-time housewives. Some aspire to full-time continuous employment careers. However, for many the ideal is a balance best achieved by working part-time and remaining the main homemaker.

New gender issues have arisen as a result of changes since the 1960s.

- Men are facing stiffer competition for entry into, then to progress in, middle-class careers.
- Economic restructuring has denied working-class males much of

their former employment. Working-class jobs that were always considered more suitable for women – in retail and hospitality for example – have become more plentiful. An outcome is said to be a crisis in working-class masculinity which is no longer rewarded in the labour market.

- Since the 1970s birth rates in most modern societies have sunk beneath the level required to replace the populations. This is now accentuating population ageing (see below) and could leave gaps in the labour market that can be filled only by immigration. Fears of being 'swamped' might be replaced by competition among Western countries for, amid an overall shortage of, potential immigrants.

- Rates of divorce and separation, births outside marriage and single parenthood have all risen. These changes have contributed to widening economic inequalities. There are more households in which two adult earners in middle-class jobs pursue scarcely inter- rupted, full-time employment careers. Simultaneously working-class women have faced an acute shortage of reliable male breadwinners. The men find themselves unwanted in the labour market and also in the family. Working-class women who are single parents may 'make-do' on welfare, if permitted to do so, or take low paid jobs where their earnings are topped-up with tax credits to the minimum level that the state deems tolerable. The answer cannot be that the women should become better qualified. As we have seen, girls now out-perform boys throughout education. It is now males who are relatively under-qualified.

RACE AND ETHNICITY

Races, Ethnic Groups and Nations

Nowadays most sociologists prefer to write about ethnic rather than racial groups. It is a common practice to set the word 'race' in inverted commas. The intention is to distance the writer from racist beliefs. It is impossible to dispense with the term 'race' while some people hold racist views, and even if they do not, they may still act as if they did. Beliefs and actions that are justified by the view that there are different human races, and that these differences justify different treatment in economic, political and social life, are called 'racist'.

Ethnic groups share a distinctive culture and a common identity. They believe that they are a common people, wider than family and kin. They are most likely to be united by some mixture of language, religion, dress, diet and, most fundamentally, a common history, real or imagined. We are all ethnic, and we are all minorities within the human species.

An ethnic group which aspires to or which has achieved statehood is called a nation. During the twentieth century the nation state came to be regarded as the normal sovereign (subject to no superior power) political unit. Hence, the title of the United Nations. In nation states there is always a titular majority. The United Kingdom would be an exception (does anyone identify as a 'United Kingdomer'?) except that there are alternative names for the territory and the titular majority (Britain and British).

A state may take its title from a territory rather than a particular nation. This has been common. With the passage of time (probably many generations) those born in the territory may become a nation, as has happened to Americans, Canadians and the populations of the Latin American states. In Africa nation-building is still in process. The states into which most of Africa was divided by colonial powers were the homes of more than one ethnic group. Territorial states may break-up before nation-building has succeeded as has happened to the former Czechoslovakia and Yugoslavia (both multi-ethnic states were created after the First World War). These break-ups have created new titular majorities and new minorities: there are Slovaks in the present-day Czech Republic and Czechs in Slovakia. Kosovo, which was part of Serbia within Yugoslavia, declared itself an independent country in 2008, creating a Serb minority in Kosovo whereas Kosovars had previously been a minority within Serbia.

The pure nation state, where the entire population belongs to the titular majority, is a fiction, a sociological ideal type, but in particular places and at particular times it has been an ideal of the governments, maybe expressing the wishes of the majority populations. There was considerable ethnic cleansing (a term first used with approval) during the wars that accompanied the break-up of Yugoslavia in the 1990s, and the de facto secessions of Abkhazia and South Ossetia from Georgia, and Nagorno Karabakh (with its mainly Armenian population) from Azerbaijan in the early-1990s. A minority may move voluntarily into the state where the people are the titular majority, but there is usually a mixture of push and pull. Minorities may feel that where they live is their real homeland. They may try to secede and become independent states, or join their territory to that of the state in which they are in the majority. Their current state is likely to resist and offer minority rights (use of the minority's language in local government and education, for example). The government usually knows that secession will create new minorities, like the Georgians who lived in Abkhazia and South Ossetia before these territories declared independence.

Minorities may be content with their minority status, especially if they have migrated into the host country. In this case they may eventually assimilate and become part of the titular majority, which is most likely if mixed marriages become common. An ethnic group which retains its identity while separated from its homeland is called a diaspora. Some ethnic groups have more members outside than resident within the territories where they are the titular majorities: Jews and Armenians, for example.

Confusingly, the term 'nationality' has a double everyday meaning. A nation is an imagined community. Nationality may refer to membership of such a group, but it is also the term used for the state of which a person is a citizen. Members of a variety of ethnic groups and nationalities may be citizens (nationals) of the same state. Forthwith, for purposes of clarity, we shall call this 'citizenship'.

In theory it is possible to conceive a purely civic state where there is no titular nationality, but over time the residents are most likely to become a nation. There are multi-ethnic states (Switzerland and Canada for example) but French and English speakers in Canada regard themselves as Canadians, and the Italians, Germans and French in Switzerland regard themselves as Swiss. Ethnicity and nationality can be multilayered. One can be both English and British. It used to be possible to be Soviet and Russian. Hyphenated identities are possible: Irish-American, Polish-American and so on. This flexibility allows for the gradual formation of new nations. In the future, a distant future, European could become a powerful identity throughout the European Union. It would be unnecessary for people to cease to be British, Germans, Poles and so on. People can activate different identities depending on the circumstances. When in Scotland I feel English, British when in France and maybe European when in America.

The term cosmopolitan has more meanings than nationality. It can refer to a person who does not identify with any ethnic group or nation but with the whole of humanity, or a person with an ethnic/national identity who does feel aligned to any state (equally comfortable, at home, in any part of the world). Both are exceptional cases. Cosmopolitan may also describe a territory, which may be an empire containing many nationalities, all formally equal (the Austro-Hungarian Empire was cosmopolitan), or a city in which diverse nationalities and ethnic groups are welcome. Cosmopolitan cannot be a description of a nation state, but a pure civic state would necessarily be cosmopolitan.

Race, nationality and ethnicity are complex topics. There are more examples of ethnic relations, each with its own particularities, than ethnic groups. These relationships always depend on the character of the ethnic groups, and the history of their relationship. It is misleading to suppose that the character of ethnic relations in one society will apply anywhere else. All countries have internal ethnic relations. Countries share this in common along with the fact that each country's ethnic relations have features that make these relations special, different from ethnic relations in other countries.

As with class, sociology uses the terms sex and gender; and ethnicity, nationality and citizenship, in ways that are congruent with their everyday meanings, but with greater precision. Sociologists are usually far more confident in placing people into classes, separating their sex and gender characteristics, and identifying their ethnicity and nationality, than the individuals themselves. In Britain today most people hesitate and are cautious if they do not refuse outright to place themselves in any social class. The same applies with ethnic groups. Mike Savage and his colleagues (2005) asked a sample of 182 respondents who all lived in mainly middle-class areas within Greater Manchester which ethnic groups they belonged to. Among those who gave any response to this question, 45 per cent said 'none': they regarded ethnicity as a feature of minorities rather than the majority population. Twenty-nine per cent gave their ethnicity as 'white' and another 4 per cent said 'Caucasian'. They were evidently conflating ethnicity with race. Six per cent gave their ethnicity as English and 4 per cent as British. Smaller percentages identified as Irish, Scots and others. According to sociology's definitions, most of the sample would have been English or British.

Race, Colonialism and Capitalism

Ethnic divisions and relations have existed throughout human history. It will now be evident that these divisions and relationships can take numerous forms. An encyclopedia would be necessary to review comprehensively even ethnic relations in modern times.

Ethnic groups may or may not be physically distinguishable, but when Europeans started to build overseas empires they colonised physically different (darker-skinned) populations. The colonised people were subordinated by their imperial rulers. This was the context in which scientific theories about racial differences were developed. The theories helped to justify colonial rule (the so-called 'white man's burden') and even the enslavement of the allegedly inferior people. This also applied to the treatment of the indigenous people of North America, Australia and New Zealand who were eventually out-numbered, forced from their land, which destroyed their economies, and undermined their cultures and ways of life. The indigenous people were neither colonized, nor embraced and absorbed into the European settlers' societies and cultures.

Race became a major issue for European and American sociology in the 1950s and has remained so ever since. The contexts were somewhat different, but with a common racial dimension. In the USA slavery had been abolished following the civil war which ended in 1865 with victory for the Republic, but a formal colour bar remained in force in much of the American South, and blatant racial discrimination remained rife throughout the entire country. During the 1950s a civil rights movement began to mobilise in the USA. European countries that had built and were dismantling empires by the 1950s, granting independence to former colonies, were by then experiencing rising inflows of migrants from past and present colonial lands. Race relations thus became a public issue in all the relevant countries: whether and how to control the inflows, and whether and how to ensure equitable treatment for those who had arrived and settled legally. Sociology needed to explain why these race relations were posing special difficulties (see Banton, 1997; Rex, 1970; Smith, 1986). Most, though not all, of the explanations were equally plausible in Europe and North America; the recent immigrant status of non-whites in Europe was the exception. It was pointed out that earlier waves of white immigrants – Irish and Jews entering Britain for example – had encountered hostility and discrimination (Patterson, 1963). However, the consensus among sociologists was that 'race' made the new immigrant-host relationships different and comparable to America's race relations.

- Research conducted at the end of the Second World War, seeking to understand how the Holocaust could have happened, had identified an authoritarian personality type, a product of strict upbringing, that was predisposed to prejudice, saw all social relationships in hierarchical terms, was prone to scapegoating, and found non-whites and immigrants convenient targets. If not these minorities, according to this theory, some other group would have been selected (see Adorno et al., 1950). This left open the question of why the non-whites had been chosen.
- One theory, plausible in both Europe and America, was that racist beliefs and attitudes were responsible. Science might have rejected racial theories, but it had not necessarily eradicated the beliefs among lay people. It was argued that the belief that non-whites were 'inferior' had become deep-seated in the dominant cultures in Europe and North America. Hence the ability of politicians to 'play the race card'. Even people who had intellectually rejected racial theories could continue to think and act in racist ways. An outcome was said to be 'institutionalised' racism – discriminatory ways of speaking and acting becoming the norm to which people were expected to conform in workplaces and neighbourhoods.

- A related theory, which has gathered increasing support in sociology, was that the status accorded to colonial peoples in Europe, and African-Americans in the USA, was due to the former's countries having been colonised, and the latter having been taken to the Americas as slaves. Historically the people had been subordinate, weaker than whites, and the societies from which they came were still weak in the global economic, political and military systems. Ethnic relations within countries were seen as reflecting global relations and inequalities between countries and their people. Over decades and centuries it seemed possible that their perceived 'inferiority' had been 'internalised' within the non-whites' cultures. Individuals from the minority groups would not necessarily suffer from low personal self-esteem or lack confidence in themselves, but they could still regard their ethnic groups as 'deficient' or 'inferior' vis-à-vis whites, thereby rendering themselves collectively unable to generate the cultural resources to demand and command respect and equal treatment.

The influence of Marxism in sociology between the 1960s and 1980s made it inevitable that the role of capitalism in the development of race relations would be interrogated. Europe's overseas empires had been built during the development of capitalism. Immigrants from the colonies had entered mature capitalist countries. Slavery in the USA, and subsequent black-white relationships, had developed in the context of American capitalism.

Slavery was not invented by capitalism. It had been practised in Ancient Greece and Rome, and earlier, and it was practised in Africa prior to European colonisation. However, it was possible to argue that capitalism gave race relations, and ethnic relations more generally, an unusually exploitative character. Slavery was not capitalism's preferred relationship of production. 'Free' wage labour was found to be more efficient and effective. The resort to slavery in the Americas was because, at the relevant time, it was impossible to attract the required numbers of free workers to the sugar and cotton plantations. That said, the form of chattel slavery that was practised, in which slaves were the property of their owners and had no recourse to law, was unusually harsh by historical standards.

Colonies were used not so much as a source of labour, but as a source of treasure and raw materials – originally gold and silver, then foodstuffs, cotton and 'ethnic' manufactures. In these ways it can be argued that capitalism systematically under-developed the economies of colonised countries (Frank, 1969). After the Second World War colonial immigrants were a reserve army for European employers. The immigrants could be hired on terms and conditions that were being rejected by the white populations in affluent, fully employed capitalist countries. Race divisions were a barrier to working-class solidarity (Castles, 1973). There were identical arguments about gender divisions, and in each case a reply was that the divisions were not created by employers alone but equally by the exclusionary tactics of patriarchal males and the white working class. Similar processes were confining non-whites to the least attractive types of housing.

Ethnic Relations in a Global Age

Race/ethnic relations look rather different today than in the 1950s and 1960s. Western countries have made racial discrimination illegal. The civil rights movement in the USA, alongside the fear aroused by urban riots, led America to introduce positive action programmes to try to compensate for centuries of discrimination. Positive action meant making extra efforts to recruit African-Americans into decent jobs, and granting college admission to applicants with lower grades than were required by whites. These measures have made a difference. At the same time, there have been equally important contextual changes.

The key change here is not that Western economies have become post-industrial. The world has become post-colonial and one consequence has been the exposure of conflicts between 'tribal' groups in the new independent states of Africa, in Sri Lanka, India, Pakistan and elsewhere. We are also in the post-Cold War era which has unfrozen and exposed ethnic conflicts in the Balkans and Caucasus. The globalisation of communications has relayed these conflicts onto global TV screens. Fifteen new independent states have been created in place of the former Soviet Union. All these new states are (or were) multi-ethnic: the countries of the South Caucasus became less multi-ethnic following the post-independence secessions and population movements. Nation-building has had to start from scratch in some of the new states. Until 1991 there were no Kazakhstanis, Uzbekistanis and their equivalents in the other ''stans'. There were Kazakhs and Uzbeks and so on, but in 1991 these became just the largest of numerous ethnic groups in the new states where they were the titular nationalities. New Russian minorities have been created in all the new independent states of the former-USSR, except in Russia itself where people from the Caucasus and Central Asia have become foreigners.

One aspect of globalisation has been increased flows of people, generally from poorer to richer countries, but in the former Soviet Union there has been an additional movement – back to the homelands where the migrants are the titular majorities. The richer countries that have received economic migrants include Western Europe, North America and Australia, but this

flow has also taken people into Russia and Kazakhstan, and some Middle
Eastern states (Dubai and Egypt for example). Unfreezing conflicts has led
to wars and refugees (asylum seekers) along with victims of political per-
secution, many from Afghanistan, Iraq, Iran and Africa. The West's race
relations look different when set in this new global context. An indicator
of the change is that many courses on race and ethnic relations have been
retitled as courses on migration (Castles and Miller, 2003).

The USA continues to receive immigrants from all over the world,
alongside a strong upsurge of 'Latinos' (from Latin America), many
crossing the USA–Mexico border legally or illegally. The ethnic mix in the
USA is changing. Spanish is already the most common first language in
California.

All West European countries are now net immigration states. They
continue to attract migrants from all over the world, especially from
former colonies, but are experiencing a new inflow from the new (in 2004
and 2007) EU member states. Most travel initially as pendulum migrants,
intending to return home, but after returning they may repeat the trips.
Some settle: this always depends on the kinds of jobs and accommodation
that they obtain, and whether they form romantic attachments. In 2012
migration into all the old (pre-2004) EU member states from anywhere
else within the EU became unrestricted, and the westward flow seems
certain to continue for as long as salary differences persist: workers generally earn at least twice as much in the West as they could expect at home.
Up to now most of these migrants have filled 'gaps' in the workforces: they
have been under-employed relative to their own qualifications, and paid
less than locals doing similar work. In the future it is likely that university
graduates who studied in the West under the EU Erasmus programme,
and who speak and write English, French and German just as well as
locals, will compete for graduate jobs. An effect has been to decouple race
from migration issues: the new migrants into Western Europe are white
Europeans.

The EU itself is a sociological problem: a very large problem with an
ethnic dimension. Originally and most basically the EU has been a single
market. Most of the national governments decided that this market would
be most effective with a single currency. This eliminates transaction costs
(the cost of exchanging currencies) and also eliminates the uncertainties of
fluctuating exchange rates. However, the effective operation of the single
currency is likely to require pooling other powers, including fiscal economic management (national taxation and government spending). Will
this strengthen European solidarity and identity or lead to a resurgence of
nationalism in opposition to rule from Brussels (or Frankfurt in the case
of the European Central Bank)? Will migrants from elsewhere in the EU

be recognised as having the same claims as nationals on jobs, housing and welfare budgets in the countries to which they move?

We have further evidence from recent times that ethnic relations within countries are sensitive to international relations between countries. The break-up of the Soviet Union and the globalisation of capitalism led Francis Fukuyama (1992), an American political scientist, to envisage (sceptically) 'the end of history' as the market economy, capitalism and Western-type democracy spread throughout the world. Some expected the twenty-first century to become the American century. Global trends have confounded any such hopes and expectations. Russia and China, and all the new Central Asian states, have opted out in favour of managed markets and democracies. There has been resistance to the spread of Western ways into some countries. Samuel Huntington (1996), another American political scientist, responded to the end of the Cold War by forecasting a new clash of civilisations, mainly Christian versus Islamic. In some Islamic countries (Saudi Arabia, Iraq, Iran, Pakistan and Afghanistan) there is opposition to the Westernisation of their lands. Their fight back has led to a wave of international terrorism, as it is experienced in the West. Muslims in Western countries complain of an outbreak of Islamophobia – the treatment as suspicious of anyone who looks Islamic. Paradoxically, there could be positive outcomes for these ethnic minorities from the global empowerment of the groups and their cultures.

In the USA an outcome of the equal opportunity laws and positive action programmes dating from the 1960s has been an expansion of a Black middle class, but African-Americans in general have remained a disadvantaged group. Meanwhile (non-white) immigrants from Asia have been progressing up America's socio-economic structure. In the UK, Indian and Chinese pupils now out-perform whites in education and are also moving up the class structure. Meanwhile, Afro-Caribbeans, Pakistanis and Bangladeshis continue to under-perform at school. So far, we have lacked a plausible explanation. A possibility is that ethnic minorities gain confidence and respect according to the positions of their original countries in a global context. China and India have historic cultures that command respect, and these countries have now become global economic powers. Ethnic groups with backgrounds in Africa and the Caribbean do not have comparable cultural assets on which to draw. The attention currently being accorded to Islam (even if its 'fundamentalists' are regarded as a threat) could have eventual benefits for the Muslim minorities in Western countries.

Colonial immigrants who have entered Europe have done so with somewhat different aspirations. Indians have not wished to be assimilated but to integrate while preserving their own culture, thus making the receiving societies more multi-cultural. Africans and Caribbeans have not brought comparable cultures and ways of life that they wish to retain. They have simply wanted to assimilate, but up to now this has proved impossible because the majority populations regard them as different. An outcome has been the formation of new ethnic identities and cultures such as Black British.

Can multiculturalism work? In 2010 the German Chancellor, Angela Merkel, pronounced multiculturalism a failure in Germany. An obstacle in Europe is that the groups who were there first regard themselves alone as the true, unhyphenated French, Germans, British and so on.

Post-colonial Sociology

Just as feminists have accused mainstream sociology of being 'malestream', critics have accused Western sociology of privileging a Western view of the world. These critics have targetted the treatment of other societies as 'undeveloped' and 'backward', and we have seen that the global context is liable to impact on ethnic relations within countries. Edward Said (1978) claims that Western orientalism presents a heavily distorted view of the East. A response has been a post-colonial sociology offering, to paraphrase Franz Fanon (1967), the view of 'the wretched of the earth'.

Once again, this raises the question of whether there can be an objective view, or whether sociology must dissolve into a variety of competing standpoints. One suggestion is that there might be a privileged position similar to that occupied by subalterns in Europe's colonial armies. Subaltern was the highest rank in these armies that was available to locals. The ranks in these armies were mainly recruited locally while the officers were all European. Subalterns, by virtue of their positions, had access to the views of both officers and men. Could sociology construct an equivalent position? A problem is that subalterns retained access to the worlds of officers and ranks only on condition of silence. Speaking out would have closed off access to one or both milieux. The subaltern position is not available to sociology because 'speaking out' is part of the mission.

OTHER DIVISIONS

Other divisions cannot perform as much work for sociology as class, gender and ethnicity. This is either because the other divisions are socially constructed to a lesser extent, or lack the same capacity to become public issues.

Age

All life stages are socially constructed to some extent but children lack the social awareness to speak out, though others may claim to speak on their behalf. By the time they reach the youth life stage, cohorts are divided by class, gender and ethnicity and they are a stream, young only temporarily, whereas gender and ethnicity are usually lifelong statuses, and people tend to remain in the same social classes throughout their adult lives.

Later life is different. Once again, everyone is part of a stream, just passing through, but later life lasts for as long as members of the age group live. They have no futures that may be different and better. Later life today lasts longer than in the past, so there are more people in this life stage. There are class, gender and ethnic divisions among older people but there are matters on which they can all agree. These include improving state pensions and other cash benefits for the retired, and adequate funding for other services that they are likely to use – health care, public transport, certain leisure facilities and broadcasting. On the retirement age they can agree on the need for choice so that those who wish to do so can draw their pensions from a relatively early age, while others who wish to do so can work for as long as they wish.

Age discrimination has been made unlawful in Western countries – a further extension of social democracy making full citizenship rights available to everyone. This legislation is most likely to prove useful to older people. Young people can be rejected for jobs or promotion because they lack relevant experience. It is more difficult to justify rejecting older people who insist that they are as mentally and physically capable as ever. Older people can insist that their needs for medical treatment that will extend their lives for a few years, maybe just a few months, and improve the quality of the rest of their (short) lives, be given equal priority to the claims of younger people who have the chance of a longer lifetime that might be saved or improved in quality.

Voting intentions at the time of the UK 2010 general election show that age had become as important as social class in predicting party choices (see Table 5.1). The over-55s, and especially the over-65s, were more likely to vote Conservative and less likely to vote Liberal Democrat than other age groups. In contrast, the Liberal Democrats were most successful in attracting support among the under-35s. Labour support was more evenly spread across all age groups. Table 5.1 also shows that the older the age group, the more likely people were to actually turn out and cast their votes. The 'grey vote' has become politically efficacious. Politicians of all parties are keen to win senior citizens' support.

Irrespective of whether young people themselves protest or applaud, the

Table 5.1   Age and voting intentions, 2010 UK general election (in percentages)

	18–24	25–34	35–44	45–54	55–64	65 and over
Conservative	30	35	34	34	38	44
Labour	31	30	31	28	28	31
Liberal Democrat	30	29	26	26	23	16
Other	9	7	9	12	12	9
Turnout	44	55	66	69	73	78

Source: MORI.

manner in which youth has recently been socially reconstructed is an issue for sociology. In the 1950s and 1960s the main issues addressed (forced onto sociology's agenda by the weight of public concern) were rising levels of juvenile delinquency and the new commercialised youth cultures that were being formed. Today the issues concern the extension of youth. The life stage has been extended downwards as a result of the marketing of youth music and fashions to children, leading to charges that children are being prematurely sexualised. The upward extension of youth is the result of young people remaining longer in education, taking longer to establish themselves in employment (across the EU27, 29 is now the first age when a majority of the age group is in full-time permanent jobs), later marriage and parenthood. Jim Arnett (2005), an American sociologist, claims that a new 'emerging adulthood' life stage has been created. These developments do not affect young people only. Will they be able to work long enough to save enough for their own retirement? Will there be enough workers to support simultaneously the retired and new cohorts of children and young people?

Sexuality

This division has become part of sociology's agenda as a result of gays, lesbians and bisexuals (GLBs) 'coming out' from the 1960s onwards and demanding the same rights and respect as heterosexuals, and succeeding in so far as sexuality has become another illegal ground for discrimination (alongside, gender, ethnicity and age). The issue has also become sociological as a result of Michel Foucault's (1926–1984) claim that before 1870 there were no homosexuals (a claim that is not generally accepted by the GLB movements). Foucault claimed that before 1870 there were people who committed homosexual acts, which might be approved, tolerated or criminalised depending on time and place, but that *the* homosexual was constructed only as part of a scientific mania for classifying humanity into races, according to their intelligence, and their propensity to commit crime (indicated by the shape of the skull and facial appearance) (Foucault, 1976). Most GLBs say that they simply 'are' whereas Foucault's claim suggests that they have internalised identities pre-constructed in a particular historical context.

'Queer' theory seeks to queer, to disturb, our normal ways of seeing things including hetero-normativity – the assumption that heterosexuality alone is normal. These normal views of the world also include the connections between male, masculinity and heterosexuality, and the female equivalents. 'Queer' theory invites us to regard any combination as possible and equally natural. Sociology is hospitable to, and indeed encourages, disturbing views of the world (views that challenge everyday common sense), but it is doubtful whether there can be a GLB standpoint that is as comprehensive (affecting experiences in all areas of life) as class, gender and ethnicity. Estimates of the size of the GLB population in the UK range from around 1 per cent (living with) to around 12 per cent (ever been attracted to). Sexuality can make a difference to us all, in most parts of our lives, only if we regard not only family relationships, but also relations at work, in politics, throughout education and so on, as predicated on heterosexual assumptions, in which case sexuality would be a system that constrained us all, all the time, to act 'normally'. One might expect such processes to disadvantage GLBs but this does not appear to be the case since survey evidence suggests that they are over-represented among higher education students and graduates, and in higher-level occupations. Why this should be so is, of course, a legitimate topic for sociological enquiry. It may be no more than a specialist topic, or the route to understanding one of the foundations of modern social life.

Health and Disability

Suppose we constructed society from the premise that all institutions, all buildings, all workplaces and all public open spaces should be designed so that it would not be a disadvantage to be blind, deaf or confined to a wheelchair, or with an IQ test score indicating subnormality. It would no doubt prove impossible to find a design that would accommodate everyone, but more than at present could be accommodated. Of course, there would be costs and inconvenience for the majority, which serves to demonstrate that the barriers and the threshold of health that is required to be fully included are at least partly socially constructed.

Nineteenth-century science classified humanity into different races, devised ways of measuring genius and subnormality, discovered born criminal types and sexual deviants, and devised treatments and cures whenever possible. Otherwise the solution was some form of care, maybe involving incarceration. Residential accommodation and sheltered employment for the blind, deaf and physically impaired were provisions for which the recipients were expected to be grateful. GLBs may object to suggestions that their 'perversions' should be treated. The disabled are more likely to regard this as the best outcome, which shows that their handicaps are only partly socially constructed. They can still argue that more could be done to include rather than exclude those with conditions that cannot be treated.

Demonstrations outside parliament by the disabled cause more embarrassment than inconvenience to politicians and the public. Sociology is less reluctant to provide a platform for these voices. Sociology is necessarily a disturbing subject, always challenging everyday views which help to make people's lives comfortable.

CONCLUSIONS

Why is sociology today considering more social divisions than in the 1950s? There are three possible answers, and each may be part of the explanation.

- *Detraditionalisation.* A long-term process of detraditionalisation which began with the Enlightenment in the seventeenth and eighteenth centuries, when all truth claims began to the subjected to reason, is said to be accelerating (Giddens, 1991, 1992). The fact that something is customary, or that a statement is something that people have always believed, cease to be accepted as sufficient. This is said to explain how age differences, sexuality and the significance of disabilities have become exposed to question.
- *Post-industrialism.* It is argued that economic issues, and hence class divisions, used to be considered all-important, whereas we are now in an era where people can make more lifestyle choices, and ethnic minorities, women, the disabled and so on all seek to become full participants.
- *Post-modernity.* The term post-modern is used in several different senses. Here it negates the modernist claim that reason will lead humanity to agreed and correct answers. One version of the post-modern mind rejects the validity claims of all 'grand narratives' and insists that there can be different views of any situation, and different

interpretations of any body of evidence, and that all can be equally correct. Hence the demands of non-heterosexuals, the disabled and people in later life that their views be accorded equal respect.

Chapter 7, on research methods, takes up the issue of whether sociology can establish a single, correct reading and explanation of events.

6. What are societies made of?

INTRODUCTION

Margaret Thatcher, UK Prime Minister throughout the 1980s, became famous (notorious really) among sociologists by declaring that there was no such thing as society, only individuals and families. She was tired of hearing society blamed for crime and other problems. Her view was that individuals were responsible, and needed to accept responsibility for their own actions.

It is true, of course, that without individuals there could be no society, but this is like observing that without chemicals there could be no biological organisms. However, organisms can be seen and touched. A society's existence cannot be demonstrated in this convenient way.

If asked to describe their subject matter sociologists have usually started off with one of two answers.

- Some liken a society to a building, a structure, or a machine of inter-locking parts (a system). The structure or system is said to be there before we are born. It awaits us. We live our lives inside the structure and our lives are governed by it.
- The alternative response has been to say that societies are built out of the actions of individuals and the relationships that they form with others.

These different views have been summarised as 'society makes man (sic)' and 'man makes society'. The former regards a society as an external reality with an independent existence. Individuals' lives are shaped by society. The latter contends that societies are created and maintained only through the actions of their members, and that without this constant maintenance work so-called structures would crumble, so-called systems would seize-up, and might then be replaced by alternatives. In 1971 Alan Dawe declared that there were in fact two sociologies: a sociology of social structure and a sociology of social action. We need to decide what society is in order to select appropriate methods for its investigation. Should we discard one definition, retain both while keeping them apart, or try to blend them together? These questions cannot be bracketed-off into a specialism called 'theory'. Anyone who treats sociology seriously, who tries to do it well, must have at least a provisional answer (always subject to revision).

SOCIETY AS A STRUCTURE OR SYSTEM

Émile Durkheim and Social Facts

Durkheim (1858–1917) had a crystal-clear, unambiguous answer to 'What is society?' Durkheim argued that a society was composed of 'social facts', and these facts were sociology's proper and exclusive subject matter. Durkheim became Europe's first Professor of Sociology in 1895, and he was determined to establish sociology as an autonomous discipline in which sociologists would be respected as experts, just like other scientists. For this to happen Durkheim believed that sociology needed a subject matter that was clearly separate, and which was not dealt with by neighbours such as psychology and history. Reductionism in sociology means breaking-up Durkheimian social facts into the behaviour of individuals, then seeking explanations at an individual level. Durkheim was aggressively anti-reductionist. Social facts were said to have an independent existence. Durkheim's social facts included suicide *rates*, crime *rates*, unemployment *rates* and so on. One social fact was to be explained through other social facts, not by reference to individual psychology. Durkheim wrote a short book, *The Rules of Sociological Method* (1895), to show how this should be done. He wrote another book, *Suicide* (1897), to illustrate his method. Durkheim had noted that suicide rates, and other rates, tended to remain stable from month to month, and often from year to year within societies (countries) while varying considerably between societies, and sometimes changing within a society over a longer term, Durkheim wanted to separate the explanation of *rates,* that is, the propensity of a population to commit crime or suicide, or their risks of unemployment, from explanations of *how and why particular individuals* became part of these rates.

Durkheim's view was that social facts were not the outcomes of the actions of numerous individuals who might have disparate motivations and objectives, but had an external existence coupled with the power to impose themselves on individuals with a moral force. Birth rates are an example. Women and couples will make their own decisions on the number of children to procreate and rear. Some will decide to have larger families than others. However, they will all be influenced by social norms (everyday views) specifying the most appropriate size of a family, and the moral force of this kind of norm will keep the rate predictable and steady. The norm, and hence the birth rate, may change over time, which will need a sociological explanation: it will not be the result of individuals and couples all spontaneously but coincidentally deciding to change their behaviour.

Durkheim explained variations in suicide rates in terms of variations in the strength of social relations that bound individuals into their societies. By relating suicide rates to other rates – of religious affiliation and participation, marriage and divorce/separation – Durkheim tried to illustrate the power of his method of sociological analysis and explanation. Suicide was commonly regarded as the most individually prompted of all actions. If he could use suicide to illustrate the power of sociology, Durkheim believed that the subject would earn the respect and recognition to which it was due. Individual factors could help to determine 'who' committed suicide, just as individual differences will play a role in deciding who becomes unemployed or who goes to university. However, individuals make employment decisions, in so far as they have scope for choice, within labour markets where there are predetermined numbers of jobs. Likewise young people decide whether or not to go to university, in so far as they can choose, in a context where the total number of university places may be predetermined, and where they may or may not have alternative opportunities (to take jobs, for example), and where only some can afford the fees and other costs that are involved.

Durkheimian social facts can be shown to be related to other social facts in a way that creates a social structure which precedes individuals in the sense that it is there before they are born, or before they enter the life stages where they make their decisions. This kind of social structure can be likened to a building within which people live their lives while leaving the structure intact, and the kinds of lives that they can choose are ultimately constrained by what the 'building' has to offer.

We can best understand the language that Durkheim used and the positions that he adopted if we set Durkheim in his own historical context. He was writing in the late-nineteenth and early-twentieth centuries. Half a century previously, his fellow Frenchman, Auguste Comte, had coined the term sociology and intended this subject to become the authoritative science of society. In the 1890s there were still no sociology courses or departments anywhere in Europe, and the possibility of developing a *science* of society was hotly disputed. Durkheim shared Comte's aspiration, but believed that Comte's own work had been speculative rather than scientific, and therefore unpersuasive. Durkheim wanted sociology to adopt what he took to be the methods of the established sciences which were to observe and measure 'facts', then establish connections between them. Durkheim also felt that it was necessary to demonstrate beyond dispute that social facts were 'things in themselves' that were not and could not be dealt with by any other discipline. As noted above, he believed that suicide, usually regarded as one of the most personally motivated of all acts, would seal his case. Alongside this, Durkheim shared the view of Comte and other nineteenth-century writers that history was being driven forward by forces over which individuals had no control. Old ways of rural life were being swept aside. Old ruling elites were being challenged and toppled. Durkheim, like Comte, Marx and others, wanted to identify the social forces that were changing Europe, and he intended to show that this could be done scientifically.

All sociology's founding fathers were at least tacitly Durkheimian, though none expressed their conception of the social as clearly, systematically and vigorously as Durkheim himself. They all recognised, as did Durkheim, that actors needed to be suitably motivated: in Comte's case by theological, metaphysical or scientific thinking; for Marx by class consciousness and conceptions of class interests; and for Weber by traditional or rational orientations to life. Durkheim's social facts exerted their force only by impressing themselves into individuals' minds, thereby compelling people collectively to behave in predicable ways. The evidence used by all the founders of sociology comprised regular, recurrent patterns of behaviour. In this they were at one with the nineteenth-century fact gatherers who measured material conditions (hard facts) rather than variable subjective experiences of poverty, squalor and ill-being.

It is worth stressing that Durkheim did not deny that individuals could act purposefully and exercise some control over their lives; nor did any of the other founders of sociology. Durkheim simply wanted to separate psychological from sociological issues. Psychology could explain which individuals; sociology would address overall rates of suicide, births, marriages and so on. Durkheim did not believe that people were mere puppets, directed by social forces. His argument was that sociology should concern itself only with the puppet-like aspects of people's behaviour. These aspects needed to be kept analytically separate from aspects of causation which originated within the person. Unless this separation was accomplished, Durkheim believed that sociology would remain disempowered, denied a subject matter in which it could claim expertise and authority. Nor was Durkheim denying that 'great men' (Mohammed, Napoleon, Bismarck and so on) could make a difference to the course of history. Max Weber regarded charisma (the personal power of a leader to inspire followers) as having played a significant role in history. For Durkheim this was the task of historians; to show how particular actors and events had accelerated, slowed or shaped the main flow of history which, in Durkheim's view, was inexorably towards an increasingly complex division of labour which sociology alone could explain.

A problem for the discipline is that Durkheim was trying to exclude from sociology the very parts that for many people make the subject interesting: why particular individuals commit crime, and how particular leaders and social movements make a difference. Most of us want a sociology that will explore how members of particular families and groups of friends view and experience 'social facts', and how and why they decide to respond in the ways that they do. We want a sociology that can account for some individuals progressing into universities while others, from the same backgrounds, end up in prison. If sociology had stuck rigidly to Durkheim's methods and definition of its subject matter, we would have nothing but a rather drab, statistics-based, variable sociology. There is plenty of this kind of sociology, but thankfully it has not become the whole of the discipline.

Sigmund Freud (1856–1939), Psychoanalysis and Sociology

Durkheim died in 1917. By 1950 both psychology and conceptions of the individual had changed dramatically. Durkheim's life overlapped with those of Sigmund Freud and George Herbert Mead (see below), but their ideas became widely known only after Durkheim died. The psychology from which Durkheim wished to separate sociology was rather different than psychology following the Second World War. Towards the end of the nineteenth century, psychology was measuring what were usually taken to be inborn human characteristics – intelligence, the propensity to commit crime and mental illness (which was then believed to have physical origins).

Freud was an Austrian-German who trained in medicine, specialised in neurology and became interested in hypnosis and 'talking therapies' as treatments for his patients' mental illnesses. He went on to invent psychoanalysis which was and still is both a theory and a therapy.

Freud claimed that there were three parts of the human mind, for which he invented labels:

- The *id*, the home of instincts (called libido), largely unconscious, but liable to take charge of behaviour at any time.
- The *super ego*, formed during childhood through internalising the views of those (usually parents) with whom the child had developed emotional bonds.

- The *ego*, the conscious part of the mind, regulated by the super ego through its ability to create feelings of shame and guilt. This required the ego to keep instincts (the id) under control. Freud believed that the development of 'civilisation' required instincts to be kept under tighter control than formerly, which led to increased risks of mental illness (Freud, 1930).

During his lifetime Freud became a controversial figure. Many people were shocked by their (partial) understanding of psychoanalysis. Freud was read as claiming that children experienced sexual urges, which was true only because Freud's libido encompassed all instinctive urges which enabled people to experience physical gratification, and he observed that children, like adults, could derive pleasure from stimulating their sexual organs. One body of nineteenth- and early-twentieth-century opinion regarded children as born in original sin from which they needed to be saved by chastisement, but the preferred view was of the innocence and purity of childhood. Even more outrageous was Freud's claim that children developed sexual feelings towards their parents. Freud did believe that children formed particularly strong emotional, gratifying ties with their mothers and fathers, which were eventually resolved by introjecting the parent (during the formation of the super ego), which allowed their libido to become fixated elsewhere. Psychoanalysis (the theory) claimed that hysteria and neuroses (symptoms for which neither the individuals nor science could provide a rational explanation) were caused by repressing (into the subconscious) rather than the normal resolution of sexual feelings and actions during childhood and adolescent development. Psychoanalysis (the method), recovered these repressed memories. This was the source of the clinical evidence on which the theory was based, and the cure for patients. Medicine was interested in Freud's ideas because otherwise it had no treatments or cures for 'madness' except to deposit patients in asylums.

Durkheim would surely have incorporated Freud's ideas into his own work had psychoanalysis (the theory) been available to him. Neither Freud nor Durkheim was a religious believer. Durkheim (1912) believed that worshippers were actually worshipping their society, represented by a totem, rather than God. Freud thought that God was an outward projection of the super ego. His theory explained how individuals could believe that they were receiving religious commands within their own minds as well as through a church. Freud's theory could also explain how individuals could retain a strong faith without needing to participate in regular collective acts of worship. Freud had a secular explanation of 'conscience' (the super ego). His contemporary, George Herbert Mead (see below), had a very similar explanation of conscience. These ideas, as well as Freud's insistence that children experienced libidinal urges, made him a controversial figure during his lifetime, but many of his claims have subsequently been generally accepted.

Following Freud, instead of Durkheim's statements about social facts exerting a moral force over individuals, sociologists have been able to offer more persuasive accounts of how a society's norms (expected ways of behaving) can become part of individuals' personalities. Thus people can be conforming with norms, yet doing so voluntarily. Such actions have been called 'voluntaristic'. By the 1950s Marxists and functionalist sociologists were adding Freud's ideas and thereby enhancing the credibility and explanatory power of their theories.

Herbert Marcuse (1898–1979), Marxism and Psychoanalysis

Marcuse became a hero of the student movements of the 1960s. He was a Marxist who developed new explanations of why capitalism had endured for longer than Marx expected. Part of the answer, according to Marcuse (1964), was that capitalism created false (consumer) needs or wants, which the system was able to satisfy, thus creating illusory feelings of freedom and happiness. Marcuse (1955) also drew upon Freud to argue that child rearing in the bourgeois family created super egos that exerted strong control over individuals' instincts, thereby producing passive adults who would submit to employers and their institutions. It did not appear difficult to persuade the students of the 1960s that in discarding sexual inhibitions they were helping to undermine capitalism.

Talcott Parsons (1902–1979) and the Social System

The inclusion of Freud into European social theories enabled Parsons to explain how individuals were socialised to play their allotted roles in the structural-functionalist model of the social system that he painstakingly constructed (Parsons, 1951). The model was built by identifying necessary functions that had to be performed in order for any society to endure. Following Durkheim, Parsons argued that the division of labour led progressively to the formation of institutions that specialised on performing specific functions. These functions were:

- *Adaptation* (to the natural environment), performed mainly by the economy.
- *Goal attainment* (setting goals for the society), performed mainly by the political system.

- *Integration* (ensuring that different institutions were coordinated), performed mainly by the legal system.
- *Pattern maintenance* (producing individuals with appropriate motivations), performed mainly by the family.

Each of the above subsystems (of the larger social system) could create its own sub-subsystems (firms, political parties and so on), within which there could be further functional specialisation with the AGIP (Adaptation-Goal attainment-Integration-Pattern maintenance) division of labour repeated endlessly. Pattern maintenance (alternatively called 'latency') was accomplished mainly in the family through the socialisation of children, and also by providing a haven in which adults could release pent-up emotions. Freudian theory was invoked to explain how socialisation, and hence 'pattern maintenance', were accomplished.

This was the kind of abstract grand theory against which C. Wright Mills (1959) launched his tirade (see pp. 28). It incorporated the over-socialised conception of man that Dennis Wrong criticised in 1961. Most sociologists at that time were not content with a definition of their subject matter in which actors appeared only as puppets, leaving the rest to psychology and other disciplines. They wanted a sociology that credited actors with the ability to make a difference.

Even so, today Durkheim's definition of sociology's subject matter and the research methods that he proposed are both flourishing, except that Durkheim's social facts have been renamed as factors or variables. Information and communication technologies have simplified the production of and access to large data-sets from which researchers can draw selected 'social facts' and relate them to one another. They can compare countries to see how differences in participation rates in higher education and the subject mixes are related to levels of subsequent employment and unemployment, and the closeness of match between qualifications and jobs. There are longitudinal data-sets which contain information collected from the same individuals at different points during their lives. It is possible to use this evidence to relate behaviour at, say, age 16 (attending youth clubs, membership of church groups and sports clubs, involvement in the arts) to outcomes such as risks of unemployment and criminal conviction up to age 30. Other potential causal factors (family class origins, ethnicity and gender, for example) can be controlled throughout the analysis. Students often conduct this kind of exercise as part of courses on quantitative research methods. Doing useful research of this type requires the investigator to have a hypothesis to test (like Durkheim's ideas about the strength of social bonds and suicide rates). The researcher then has to locate a suitable data-set and from it select the appropriate variables.

We can note that causation is always attributed: it can never be demonstrated. A relationship between two variables may be spurious. This applies even with longitudinal data: the hypothesised independent and dependent variables may both be controlled by a third, unexamined causal factor. There may be more than one hypothesis that can explain a relationship. In this case an investigator may seek additional evidence that will arbitrate between the competing hypotheses. Generally, a powerful theory that explains many relationships between variables is considered preferable to having as many theories (confirmed hypotheses) as there are relationships, but this is not conclusive proof that the powerful theory is right.

Supporters of these methods say that the proof is that they work. Critics remain suspicious of any explanations that make no reference to the actors' choices and intentions.

SOCIETY AS SOCIAL ACTION

Max Weber (1864–1920)

Although Weber can be said to have dealt with 'social facts', he held a somewhat different view to Durkheim on the constitution (make-up) of societies. During Weber's lifetime there was a fierce debate in Germany about whether a *science* of society was possible. Wilhelm Dilthey (1833–1911), a historian, and speaking for his discipline, rejected the idea (Dilthey, 1976). He argued that the way to explain what happened in history was to access the minds, the cultures and the spirit of the age. This has in fact remained the orthodox way of doing history. Peter Winch (1958) among others right up to the present, have rejected the idea of a social science on basically the same grounds. Winch argued that the rules, including the laws, that the members of a society observe are entirely different from the cause–effect laws of the natural sciences. People have the ability to think and to reflect on their situations, then act accordingly, which means that explanations must take a different form than in physics and chemistry.

Weber tried to adopt a mid-way position. He accepted that behaviour needed to be 'understood' (as historians insisted) but argued that this could be a prelude to and a part of a causal explanation, though he rejected the idea that there could be general laws governing history or society. Weber's technique was to identify a causal process by setting actors' meaningful behaviour in its historical context. His main example was the Protestant ethic (Weber, 1905). A Calvinist view of the world could make behaviour meaningful and explain Calvinists' responses to the business opportunities created by the concurrent expansion of trade and the possibility of adopting new ways of manufacturing. Otherwise Weber's main examples of views of the world were his contrast between the traditional (a predisposition to continue to do things in customary ways) and the rational (a predisposition to select the best means to achieve an end) (see Gerth and Mills, 1946). Rendering behaviour meaningful at an individual level as part of a sociological explanation is now called 'methodological individualism'. Weber was a methodological individualist though he himself did not use the term. This method is not the same as reducing the social to the psychological and explaining behaviour in terms of laws of psychology.

Weber did not interview any Protestants. He never conducted anything that could be called fieldwork. His method of rendering behaviour meaningful was to construct ideal types – unrealistically pure constructs of phenomena such as the Protestant ethic, the spirit of capitalism, rational action and bureaucracy. His test of a type was whether it worked in the sense of making behaviour both meaningful and explicable in causal terms. Weber's method was conceptually sophisticated, but somewhat cavalier in its use of evidence, highlighting facts that fitted the type and ignoring others. Weber simply invented states of mind which corresponded to observed behaviour (the ethic of the Protestants who developed capitalist enterprises, for example), thereby enabling the behaviour to be 'understood' as part of a causal explanation. Another invented ideal type was the rational mind of the bureaucrat. Alfred Schutz (1899–1959) was to criticise Weber's method and call for a more rigorous application of a 'phenomenological' approach (see below). Nevertheless, Weber is regarded as a founder of the 'action approach' in sociological explanation in which actors (sometimes called agents because they are mediating their social contexts) can make a difference.

George Herbert Mead (1863–1931)

Mead was a contemporary of Sigmund Freud, but neither seems to have known about or to have influenced the other. Independently they developed similar ideas. This is not unusual. Scientific discoveries and inventions are often made more-or-less simultaneously but independently. The different minds are working from the same state of knowledge, in the same historical context and looking for solutions to similar problems.

Mead worked at the University of Chicago, the main home of American sociology at that time, but he did not regard himself as a sociologist. His work was very different from that of colleagues who were conducting investigations in the city. Mead regarded himself as working at the crossroads between philosophy and psychology. In this respect he was similar to his contemporary, Charles Horton Cooley (1864–1929), who is claimed as a founder of American sociology (which has its own founding fathers) although Cooley worked at the University of Michigan, not Chicago, and positioned his own work at the crossroads of psychology, philosophy and history. Cooley invented the expression, 'the looking glass self', meaning that we see ourselves as others see us. This view was expressed independently but less elegantly, by Mead. Cooley also first used the term 'primary group' (face-to-face relationships between known persons) which could be contrasted with the formal organisation.

Mead believed that people's ability to use symbols, signs that stand for something else, language being the prime example, set them apart from other animals. He claimed that the self, self-consciousness, was a social product rather than something that would develop if individuals lived in isolation other than having their physical needs met. The languages that we learn, according to Mead, enable us to take-on the roles of other people, to imagine how they see themselves and ourselves. Mead argued that individuals internalised the views of 'significant others', that is, those who played significant roles in their lives, mainly parents in the first instance. The internalised attitudes of significant others were merged into a 'generalised other', the counterpart of Freud's super ego. This enabled the individual to conduct internal conversations between an 'I' (myself as I really am, the counterpart of Freud's ego) and a 'me' (as I imagine others see me). Thus the self (I as I really am) and self-consciousness were to be explained as products of social interaction, and in this sense a self was necessarily a socialised self – an unsocialised self was impossible.

Self-consciousness, a product of human's ability to develop and use language, was said to separate humans from other animals. This claim of human exceptionalism is now controversial because there is evidence that some other animals can think and develop new ideas (apes constructing simple tools, for instance), which implies self-consciousness, which implies that their sounds and actions have symbolic meanings among the species. Needless to say, whether humans really are exceptional animals in this respect is irrelevant to claims that the processes whereby the self and self-consciousness arise depend on the ability to use symbols.

Structural Marxists and structural functionalists have tended to incorporate Freud rather than Mead. Freud's super ego is more severe, more repressive, than Mead's relatively friendly 'me'. Mead's personality lacks Freud's id, instincts that can be repressed then at any time break-out and take control of behaviour. Unlike Freud, Mead was not trying to explain mental illnesses. Mead's 'I' has more autonomy than Freud's ego. These are probably the reasons why subsequent sociologists who have selected 'action' as the basic building block of society have tended to use Mead rather than Freud, and have named Weber as their other inspiration. They agree that structural Marxism and structural functionalism both incorporate the over-socialised model of man that was criticised by Dennis Wrong (1961).

Herbert Blumer (1900–1987) and Symbolic Interaction

Blumer took over Mead's lectures at the University of Chicago on Mead's death in 1931, and went on to build Mead's ideas into a theory that Blumer called symbolic interactionism. This theory foregrounded Mead's observation that people communicate symbolically and do not interact in the same way that physical objects impact on one another. Thus social relationships are qualitatively different than the cause–effect relationships observed in the physical sciences. Most (though not all) interaction between people is symbolic. One actor 'codes' the meanings that he or she wishes to convey into symbols (usually words, though facial expressions and physical gestures can also be used). A receiver must 'decode' the message then respond accordingly. This leaves enormous scope for misunderstandings. People must constantly try to make themselves understood, and to have their 'definition of a situation' accepted by others. Thus social reality (what is actually the case) is fragile, not a rigid social structure or system. Social reality is said to be 'negotiated'. The parties always have to try to reach agreement on 'what is the case'. Symbolic interactionists have agreed with Weber that social behaviour cannot be explained in terms of universal laws. The fact that social behaviour is basically symbolic leads to arguments that the study of signs/symbols (alternatively known as semiology or semiotics) must be at the core of sociology.

Symbolic interactionism is compatible with phenomenology. This is a philosophical doctrine originally formulated by Immanuel Kant (1724–1804), the revered German philosopher. The ideas were developed by Edmund Husserl (1859–1938) and applied to sociology by Alfred Schutz (1899–1959). The central claim is that all our knowledge is phenomenal (about things as they appear). We have no access to mind-free knowledge about things as they really are, which Kant called 'nuomena'. This raises questions about the status of all truth claims in sociology, which are taken-up in Chapter 7. Within sociology phenomenology has been treated as confirmation that actors behave according to their definitions of a situation, not the situation as it appears to anyone else, including sociologists, and that things as they really are cannot be directly apprehended by the human senses. In other words, there are no 'hard' social facts for sociology to access and study. In 1927 an American sociologist, William Isaac

Thomas, made the memorable statement (before symbolic interactionism had been born), that if men (sic) define situations as real they are real in their consequences. Hence the importance of delving into people's minds, recognising that any situation or event may look differently to any two individuals and any two social groups.

Erving Goffman (1922–1982), a Canadian-born American sociologist, did not describe himself as a symbolic interactionist or apply any other label to his work, but symbolic interactionists have claimed Goffman as one of their own. Goffman was a maverick and prolific sociologist in the 1960s and 1970s, who is seen as having pioneered a 'dramaturgical approach'. Society was likened to a theatre with scripts and roles for actors. People came on stage, interpreted their roles, and presented their selves as they wished to be seen. They could present different selves according to whether they were front or backstage. Goffman claimed that his ideas had been influenced by observations in hotels. He wrote about how individuals handle stigma, spoiled identities, and how total institutions institutionalise their inmates (make them totally dependent on the institution). He also explained how our interpretation of any act (a speech act or another type of behaviour) always depends on the context (what Goffman called the 'frame') (Goffman, 1959, 1961, 1964, 1974). We interpret speech acts differently when we know that they are part of a job interview than when the same acts occur within a conversation between friends in a cafe. All this was received as exemplary symbolic interaction analysis.

However, the most famous, and probably the most successful example of symbolic interactionist sociology was its application to deviance. In the 1960s, symbolic interactionists created a 'new criminology'. The core contention was and still is that deviance and crime are labels rather than inherent in any acts. Favoured examples have been drug use and profit-making (applauded under capitalism but a crime in Communist countries). Symbolic interactionists have sought explanations of why particular groups wish to apply these labels to acts that others consider harmless or even praiseworthy, and how some succeed in having their definitions widely accepted. They have also explored the consequences of the public application of deviant labels to individuals, and how an outcome is likely to be secondary deviance through forcing those concerned further apart from mainstream society (Becker, 1963; Lemert, 1967).

Symbolic interactionists have thoroughly enjoyed deconstructing Durkheimian social facts. They have shown how suicide rates can depend on coroners' variable interpretations of evidence, and how grieving relatives may persuade a doctor to attribute a suspicious death to natural causes. They have been able to show how official crime statistics are influenced by police recording practices: should a domestic incident be treated as a crime? They have discussed how the police can exercise discretion and issue an informal warning rather than taking things further. These police judgements have been shown to be related to the class and ethnicity of the offender. A response to the evident unreliability of official crime statistics has been to conduct surveys, such as the now annual British Crime Survey, which ask representative samples of the public about their experiences as victims. Are the crime rates thereby calculated any more accurate than police and court records? People can exercise discretion when deciding whether or not to tell investigators about incidents such as thefts within a family household, or they may have forgotten occasions when they were alarmed by anti-social behaviour.

Symbolic interactionism has always proved a student-friendly kind of sociology. It explores the experiences and views of the world of the poor, drug users, strikers and prisoners. Durkheimian social facts and Parsonian social structures are usually experienced (by sociology students) as less enthralling. Undergraduates may undertake mini-projects as part of courses on qualitative research methods in which they conduct a limited number of in-depth interviews exploring the symbolically constructed worlds of their subjects. This kind of research is popular among postgraduates for the more ambitious projects on which they base their Ph.D. theses. Such research might explore, for example, how the police and students interpret particular kinds of events, such as those that occur during student demonstrations. We can note that the value of this kind of research is magnified if it is possible, from existing quantitative evidence, to establish exactly who and how many people of those who are interviewed may be taken to represent.

Another appeal of this kind of sociology has been its insistence that all so-called structures are fragile. They retain their appearances of solidity only for as long as people continue to believe in them. Money works like money only while people retain confidence that the pieces of paper can be exchanged for goods and services. If confidence is lost, currencies are devalued and may even become worthless. When symbolic interactionism burst into sociology (in the 1960s) it appeared to open endless possibilities for renegotiating reality. The crime problem could be diminished if more offences were treated as minor misdemeanours, akin to student rags, and if society desisted from publicly labelling so many individuals as 'deviant'. Alternatively, society could be changed by imposing draconian penalties, lengthy periods of judicial incarceration, on profiteers, tax evaders and employers who could be held responsible for serious accidents at work. Some once believed that the capitalist state would crumble if delegitimised, that is, if enough people refused to accept the state's view of the world and its own role within it. Symbolic interactionists subscribe to the power of ideas – the possibility of human thought changing the world.

SYMBOLIC CAGES

Present-day sociologists, who accept that social action, interaction, and negotiated definitions of identities and situations are the basic constituents of society, are unlikely to agree with the idea that people can change things simply by mutual agreement. This claim has met a triple challenge: from within sociology (ethnomethodology), linguistics (structuralism) and the history of thought (discourses). All claim, albeit in different ways, that when we interact with one another, even when we feel that we are being creative and unconventional, we are usually compounding our subordination to existing regimes.

Ethnomethodology

This has remained a small and specialised movement within sociology. It was founded in the 1960s by the American, Harold Garfinkel (1917–2011). The term 'ethnomethodology' is meant to be construed literally. It is the study of the methods that people (ordinary people) use to agree upon what is happening around them, what is actually the case, and thereby establish a basis for orderly interaction. Talcott Parsons' social system, with its layers of subsystems, was enveloped by a single cultural system. Functionalist sociologists have sometimes treated value consensus as a condition for orderly social life. 'Value consensus' might be rephrased as 'cultural consensus'. For any social life to be possible, there must be agreement on a common language, the meanings of words, and hence our ability to agree on 'the situation out there'. Ethnomethodology emphasises that the starting point in all social encounters must be to agree on 'what is actually the case'. Unless this is agreed, nothing can be renegotiated. Ethnomethodologists regard orthodox symbolic interactionist work as hopelessly superficial. They, the ethnomethodologists, seek to delve deeper, and to uncover in everyday life what in sociology or any other academic discipline would be called domain assumptions, axioms, or a problematic – whatever is taken as 'given'. Ethnomethodologists have pioneered some distinctive research methods (Garfinkel, 1967):

- *Conversation analysis*, through which they aim to identify the implicit rules that keep conversations orderly – how people agree to take turns, and how they indicate that a turn has ended, for example.

- *Keep asking 'Why?'* People are questioned about their behaviour. Whatever they answer they are then asked, 'Why do you say that?' or 'What do you mean?' At some point the subjects are expected to become frustrated, angry, and to insist that their meanings must surely be clear, thus exposing what is ordinarily just taken for granted.
- *Disrupt expectations.* Experimenters are asked to behave in unexpected ways. For example, students who live at home have been asked to start behaving as if they were lodgers. This is expected to expose what is ordinarily expected, taken for granted, with a resident family member.

Ethnomethodology is not widely practised. Most sociologists regard it as offbeat. Conversation analysis has become part of sociology's mainstream, but otherwise ethnomethodology's distinctive methods have remained unusual. Nevertheless, ethnomethodologists claim that it is only because some things are simply taken as 'given', beyond question, that actors in specific situations are able to agree on 'what is the case', thus making orderly life, including change, possible. They proceed to argue that uncovering the 'givens' has to be a starting-point for sociology. The 'givens' permit mutually meaningful interaction, enable people to develop and adopt new ideas and relationships, whilst staying within limits on what can be agreed to be or become the case.

Ethnomethodologists claim that their methods are uncovering the true bedrock of social reality – understandings that are internalised at the same time when language and the ability to communicate are acquired. Thereafter conversations and interaction can be orderly only if common understandings are accepted and neither questioned nor breached. Paradoxically, even when we disagree and negotiate fiercely, we simultaneously confirm underlying rules of engagement.

Structuralism

This movement started in linguistics (the study of languages), then spread to other disciplines during the 1960s, initially in France, then globally. The main exponent in sociology/social anthropology (by the 1960s the boundaries were blurred) was Claude Lévi-Strauss (1908–2009). Linguists claimed to have identified similar rules of grammar in all human languages, and a favoured explanation was that the ability to acquire language is innate: that all grammars are based on a genetically programmed structure. Hence the ease with which children became competent speakers (Chomsky, 1957). We use language to think, to communicate and to form relationships with other people which, it is claimed, are all bound to be governed by the same common underlying structures as rules of grammar.

In social anthropology and sociology, structuralism (not to be confused with structural-functionalism) identifies common features of myths and social relationships that are present in different societies. It thereby demonstrates the unity of humanity: supposedly primitive savages are shown to think in much the same ways as people who regard themselves as far more civilised (Lévi-Strauss, 1969, 1972).

Structuralism was most influential in the analysis of texts, especially among scholars of literature, where before long post-structuralists were arguing that numerous interpretations of any text are possible, and that structuralists' claim to have identified the correct meaning (the underlying structure) is false. Even so, similar underlying rules (of grammar and therefore communication) which are embedded in raw human nature suggest that there are limits to our ability to negotiate definitions of situations.

Discourses

Michel Foucault (1926–1984), a Frenchman, was not a sociologist, but his books (Foucault, 1963, 1975, 1976), all dealing with the history of thought since early modern times, have been extremely influential in sociology since the 1980s. Ethnomethodology and structuralism have been noted: Foucault has really impacted on sociology. He argued that every historical era has been governed by a system of thought (called an *episteme*), within which *discourses* can be developed (rule-governed ways of thinking and speaking). Present-day societies, in Foucault's view, are *carceral* (administered) societies, governed by scientific discourses which authorise experts to keep subjects under ever-increasing surveillance and control. Foucault's books are about such modern institutions as prisons, asylums, clinics and the control of sexuality – all illustrating how experts have been given the right to diagnose, control and treat us. Much of present-day sociology, in Foucault's view, has become part of this system. The orthodox view has been that science gives people ever-increasing control over their own lives. Foucault suggests exactly the opposite: the details of our lives are being monitored and controlled to an unprecedented extent. We are followed everywhere by closed circuit TV/video cameras, our medical details, our incomes and details of how we spend our money, are all stored in databases.

Irrespective of the extent to which our lives are monitored and controlled, the proposition remains that in so far as we interact using the discourses of our era, our most creative thoughts become part of the process (the system of governance) that subordinates us to the ongoing social order. Hence the limits to the changes that might be achieved through symbolic interaction in so far as the symbols are embedded in discourses that govern the possible outcomes. The Foucauldian view is that its discourses are the real bedrock of any society. We shall see in Chapter 8 that there is a neo-Marxist critical sociology (founded by the Frankfurt School before the Second World War) which argues that an emancipatory sociology needs to begin by emancipating itself from the system of thought that has been dominant in modern capitalist societies.

BRIDGING CONCEPTS

Asking sociologists to define society is like asking natural scientists to define matter. Sociologists (like natural scientists) will agree that the issue is important and must be debated, but may ask whether a precise agreed definition is necessary. Sociologists need to engage with 'What is society?' only as far as is necessary in addressing their principal questions which are about change and stability in particular societies, and the divisions within them. The different definitions of society do not lead to wholly different answers to such questions. This is because sociologists who foreground structure admit that these structures are maintained only through the agency of (socialised) actors. Those who foreground action will agree that actions can be imagined only using socially acquired knowledge, and that actions may well meet resistance from the structure-like consequences of other people's actions. This suggests that it should be possible to reconcile sociology's two ways of defining society, and two bridging concepts have become widely used during the last 30 years.

Structuration

This term was invented by Anthony Giddens (b. 1938), probably the best internationally known of all current UK sociologists. He claims that structure and agency each presume the other, and indeed are embedded in each other. Structures are the outcomes of the actions of people who are behaving in meaningful ways. Simultaneously, an input from a society's structures is necessary for people to behave in meaningful ways since the self is a social product. Giddens (1979, 1984) calls all this structuration – a process. Structures are always being reinforced or weakened as a result of meaningful actions, and actions are always influenced by existing structures.

Structuration is not an idea that can be treated like a hypothesis and tested. Its point is that proponents of structure and agency may adopt different starting-points, but once any investigation proceeds, the complementary processes can easily be accommodated. There are 'fact-like' regularities in social behaviour. Some regularities co-exist. In other cases the presence of one diminishes the likelihood of encountering the other. These regularities cannot be ignored, but their adequate explanation is most likely to require resort to an action perspective.

Habitus

This is a concept used by Pierre Bourdieu (1930–2002), a French sociologist; probably the world's most influential and acclaimed sociologist since the 1970s when his books began to be translated and published in other languages.

Habituses are metaphorical dwellings in which we live, except that the habitus is not outside our bodies but within our minds. A habitus is said to be formed during early socialisation and consists of durable perceptions, understandings and predispositions to action. Bourdieu (1984) claimed that members of a social class tend to acquire a class-specific habitus which can contain the accumulated experience of the class. The same can be claimed of gender and ethnic groups. People are said to mix most easily and form bonds with others who possess a similar habitus. Actions are not rigidly rule-bound, but are always governed by the habitus.

Sociologists have found habitus more user-friendly than Freud's super ego and Mead's generalised other. Habitus credits actors with greater flexibility, and explains how macro-structures such as class divisions tend to be reproduced over time while being susceptible to change (Bourdieu and Passeron, 1977). However, habitus has the same vulnerability as super ego and generalised other. There is no way in which any of these postulated entities can be observed. Their existence is proposed to explain how people behave and the views they express (which can be observed). The hypothesised content of a habitus is induced from these observations, and the habitus is then said to explain the observations, which is circular and therefore unsatisfactory.

This does not mean that the habitus (or the super ego or generalised other) do not really exist, but like structuration, the concepts cannot be operationalised and directly measured. The point is that sociology, like all other sciences, needs to postulate the existence of phenomena and processes in order to explain its observations. The postulates cannot be directly 'sensed' and thereby subjected to a direct test. They are retained unless or until alternative postulates offer more powerful and plausible explanations.

CONCLUSIONS

Structure and action offer compatible and complementary explanations of how regular patterns of behaviour (Durkheim's social facts) persist over time. The action perspective can explain *how* change occurs. As regards *why* change happens, sociology has three explanations, each of which may apply in different examples of change.

- Durkheim's account of the division of labour becoming a self-perpetuating process.
- The Marxist view that different sections of a population will develop different 'definitions of the situation'. Marx emphasised the role of class conflict, but the explanation can be applied to gender, ethnic and other divisions.
- Weber did not disagree with Marx on this, but added that charismatic individuals (Calvin for example) could spread new ideas that mobilised supporters, but the character of the changes wrought, if any, would always depend on the surrounding context.

These processes will explain change within families, businesses, voluntary associations and any other subsystem (to use Talcott Parsons' language), and may occasionally spread across an entire society creating major historical transformations.

7.   Research methods

INTRODUCTION

The only effective way of learning research methods is to use them. Methods are like foreign languages in this respect. Classroom instruction alone does not produce effective communicators. This is why practicals are always at the heart of research methods courses. A research-based dissertation is invariably part of final year undergraduate work. Hands-on experience forces appreciation of the issues that arise in selecting a sample, conducting an interview, analysing a text (a newspaper story or an interview transcript, for example), and creating then analysing a quantitative data-set.

Hands-on learning may be the first step towards a career as a researcher in a university, or in a research organisation, or more likely in the research division of a commercial business, a voluntary association or a public body. However, larger numbers of former sociology students become users of research in their jobs in the public, voluntary and commercial sectors. They need to be able to assess whether the conclusions in a report can be trusted, and whether the investigators have selected appropriate methods and used them correctly. Users may also commission research, in which case they need to be able to set realistic aims and sensible guidelines. In the shorter term, for sociology students, appraising the literature in any field of the discipline requires an understanding of how evidence is created (it is created, not simply discovered). Students also need to be able to assess the confidence that can be attached to the results of different kinds of enquiry.

Sociologists invariably claim that their knowledge is superior to everyday common sense, and that their conclusions are not mere personal opinions. This chapter begins by reviewing the basis of these claims. Until the 1950s most sociologists would have based the claims squarely on their scientific methods. Subsequently the chapter introduces sociology's methods of gathering quantitative and qualitative evidence, then concludes by noting what makes sociology's methods different from those of other social sciences.

SCIENCE AND POSITIVISM

Scientific Method

Originally 'science' was another word for 'knowledge'. During the Renaissance (a movement in learning and the arts that began in Northern Italy during the fourteenth century) science became a particular kind of knowledge that was developed and recorded systematically. Scientists made systematic observations, recorded the results and then drew conclusions. This was the notion of science to which Auguste Comte (1798–1857) subscribed. Comte was the Frenchman who first used the term 'sociology' (see pp. 8–9). His sociology was scientific, he believed, because his observations identified regular patterns of co-existence and succession among social phenomena, which Comte called 'laws', the equivalent of the laws of the natural sciences. Comte described his method and his conclusions as *positivist* because he was optimistic about the benefits that would follow. He believed that his science of society would replace speculation, tradition and religion, and the outcomes would be better laws, better government, and improvements in business and social life more generally. Following Comte, in sociology a positivist has always been someone who seeks to replicate the methods of the natural sciences. Until the 1950s most sociologists (and most economists, psychologists and political scientists) were proud to regard themselves and to be recognised as positivists.

Towards the end of the nineteenth century and throughout Émile Durkheim's (1858–1917) career (see pp. 14–18), philosophers and scientists formulated a more detailed version of the scientific method. It was said to involve induction and deduction, formulating and testing hypotheses, and conducting controlled experiments when possible. From their observations scientists would induce a hypothesis (an explanation of the relationships observed). From the hypothesis they would make deductions which could be tested by making further observations. If confirmed, a hypothesis would become a law. Lower level laws would be explained by higher level laws, and the entire body of knowledge would be a theory. This was the idea of science with which Durkheim worked, and which he tried to apply in sociology.

During the 1920s and 1930s these ideas were formally set-out and further refined by the Vienna Circle, a group of philosophers who described their doctrines as *logical positivism*. They noted that some propositions could be proved by pure logic ($2 + 2 = 4$), and that evidence from observation was not required, which was not an original claim. They also insisted that 'is' and 'ought' statements had to be kept separate: that neither could be derived from the other. We shall return to this particular

doctrine, an original claim by the Vienna Circle, in Chapter 8. As regards
scientific method, their main contribution was to introduce the principle of
falsifiability. In order to be admitted into science, propositions had to be
falsifiable and, to be accepted as correct, propositions had to be validated
by sensory evidence (observations). Talcott Parsons' theory about social
systems and their functional requisites would have failed this test: no possible observation could falsify the theory. The inevitability of a proletarian
revolution 'in the long run' would also be excluded from science on the
same ground. In order to make sociology truly scientific, it appeared necessary for the discipline to become more selective about the range of propositions that it was willing to entertain. By the Second World War this was
how sociologists who wished to be considered scientists were being urged
to reorient their subject. This meant setting aside grand speculative claims
about the character of all societies and the course of human history, and
building upwards from more modest propositions that could be tested
against evidence which, in principle, allowed hypotheses to be falsified and
rejected as incorrect.

The Reappraisal of Science

Until the 1950s the orthodox view in sociology had been that there was
a scientific method and that if the social sciences could correctly identify and adopt this method, they would achieve comparable advances in
knowledge, and their pronouncements would carry the same authority, as
enjoyed by medicine and other natural sciences. By the end of the 1960s
sociology had changed. Within the discipline, the argument that people
are different, and that the social sciences' methods and explanations must
also be different from those in the natural sciences, had become ascendant
(see below). Also, the notion that there was *a* scientific method that would
enable sociology and other social sciences to develop proper scientific laws
and theories had been queried by philosophers and historians of science.

    Karl Popper (1902–1994) was an Austrian-born philosopher, a member
of the Vienna Circle, who worked in London from 1946. He accepted the
Vienna Circle's principle of falsifiability: science should admit only propositions that were susceptible to disproof by contrary evidence. Popper was
fiercely critical of closed systems of thought which, in his view, pervaded
and prevented the social sciences from progressing. A closed system is a set
of ideas that can accommodate any evidence and is therefore self-sealing.
Popper's favourite examples included psychoanalysis and Marxism. This
led Popper to become a passionate defender of 'open societies' where all
ideas could be criticised. He believed that authoritarian states which sup-
pressed dissent (like Fascism and Communism) would inevitably stagnate.

Science itself had to be open, which meant banishing self-sealing theories (Popper, 1945, 1957). A one-time student of Popper, George Soros, went on to become an extremely successful financial investor and speculator (achievements which he did not credit to Popper), but following the collapse of Communism Soros founded and funded the Central European University, and also the Open Society Institutes which were established, wherever permitted, throughout Eastern Europe and the former Soviet Union. These initiatives were intended to ensure that the transformed societies became genuine open societies.

Sociology has not banished closed systems of thought. Rather, it has become more comfortable with self-sealing views of the world: an example of self-aware strategic naivety. The reasons will become apparent in what follows. Sociology has been more comfortable with one of Popper's subsidiary arguments. This was that the corpus of scientific knowledge consists of propositions that have so far not been disproven. Popper argued that there was no special scientific method of induction – developing sound hypotheses and theories. These were always conjectures – ideas that sprang into someone's mind. Popper argued that propositions were strengthened by surviving successive efforts to disprove them. The secret of scientific progress was to admit only falsifiable propositions, which could then be interrogated rigorously by a scientific community. Deductions would be made which allowed propositions (hypotheses) to be tested. In the face of contrary evidence, propositions had to be modified, or abandoned and replaced. This was how the sciences had advanced. Nothing was ever accepted as finally true, beyond question. Truth was simply what had not yet been challenged successfully (Popper, 1963). Popper was not suggesting that this was how individual scientists worked; rather that, whether they realised it or not, progress was the result of trying to disprove ideas that their colleagues had proposed.

Sociologists have always been rather good at attacking each other's ideas, so they have had every reason to be comfortable with Popper's assurance that their attempts to falsify are scientifically sound. In contrast, the discipline has been unwilling to relinquish non-falsifiable theories. Popper's advice was to abandon the quest for laws of history: history could reveal only trends which could not be treated as scientific laws. Popperian sociology would limit itself to testable 'if-then' propositions. There would be no place for questions such as 'Why did industrialisation happen first in the West?' or 'What is society?' Fortuitously, support for retaining self-sealing theories came from work on the history of science.

In the 1960s Thomas Kuhn (1922–1996), an American historian of science, was arguing that in practice the sciences had not developed in a Popperian manner, with individual scientists critically interrogating and modifying each other's hypotheses. Kuhn (1962) argued that the natural sciences had not developed gradually and smoothly through numerous short strides, but through periods of normal science which were punctuated by scientific revolutions. For most of the time scientists were said to work within accepted 'paradigms' – accepted definitions of the problems to be addressed and the methods to be used. Scientists were not constantly sceptical and critical of each other's work. They were not perpetually questioning accepted wisdom in their subjects. Such behaviour would have prevented them securing funding for their research and would have blocked their research careers. Rather, normal scientists accepted prevailing views about what should be investigated and how. These paradigms resembled Popper's closed systems of thought. Kuhn argued that the sciences progressed through steadily accumulating knowledge within a paradigm, but that points were reached when the evidence produced became incompatible with the paradigm itself. These were revolutionary moments, when new paradigms could be proposed by great figures of the sciences such as Newton, Darwin and Einstein, which then became the bases for further periods of normal science. The revolutionary moment explained why new ideas, discoveries and inventions were often made almost simultaneously but independently. However, the key message was that scientific progress did not occur as a result of all scientists trying to become the new Newton, Darwin or Einstein, but through the relatively mundane, routine work of normal scientists. It was this work which developed knowledge within a paradigm that eventually led to revolutionary upheavals. Thus sociologists who operated within (temporarily) closed systems of thought were not enemies of intellectual progress.

Post-positivist Sociology

Since the 1960s the orthodox view in sociology has been that humans are different from inanimate objects in ways that make it inappropriate for sociology to try to emulate the methods of the natural sciences. Applying the label 'positivist' to anyone has been an implied criticism. Sociology, it is now said, must be a *social* science, with 'science' reverting to its post-Renaissance but pre-twentieth-century meaning, namely, knowledge that is different from the everyday variety in being collected and recorded systematically. Sociology has absorbed the implications of humans having consciousness – of their environments and their selves – and being able act intentionally, to decide whether or not to observe laws, traditions and normal forms of social behaviour. Max Weber's insistence that sociological explanations cannot be in terms of general laws, and must incorporate an understanding of the actors' frames of mind, which makes it possible to explain their behaviour given their circumstances and intentions, have become mainstream sociological positions. The same applies to the insistence of symbolic interactionists that the study of social behaviour must be about how people interpret signs and how they try to make their own meanings understood by others.

This post-positive position has posed new problems for sociology. If an actor's definition of a situation is a variable, that is, if many views of the situation are possible, all capable of having real consequences, and if we accept that all knowledge is phenomenal (see pp. 97–9), why does all this not apply to sociology? Must the discipline abandon all claims to objectivity, that is, access to the correct account of situations? Must sociology dissolve into a series of standpoints – feminist, post-colonial, queer, bourgeois, proletarian and purely personal? Various escapes for sociology have been proposed, but none have been embraced by the entire discipline as wholly satisfactory.

The phenomenological reduction

Phenomenology (see pp. 97–9) insists that mind-free knowledge of an external reality is impossible; that we have no means of directly apprehending things as they really are, or even proving that there actually is a real world outside our minds. When we apply this doctrine to society we recognise that for orderly social life to be possible people must somehow manage to reach agreement on 'what is actually the case'. They must establish intersubjective agreement, which phenomenology describes as a 'natural attitude', and is usually experienced by subscribers as objectively valid. People need to share a natural attitude in order to go about their daily lives, as do scientists if they are to work within a common 'discipline'. All scientific communities must agree on what is known, what is still unknown, and how such mysteries might be resolved.

A solution proposed for sociology is somehow to 'bracket out' the contributions of human minds to what is taken to be the case. This process is known as the *phenomenological reduction*. The study of social life must start with an exploration of the actors' consciousness. The minds of different actors may lead to somewhat different perceptions of what is really the case. If the minds' contributions can be identified and bracketed out, sociologists will be left with what really is the case in society out there, and their own discipline's natural attitude will be superior to those of other actors. Ethnomethodology (see pp. 102–3) is a set of methods for exploring people's minds which will expose what is ordinarily taken for granted.

These practices may offer interesting additions to knowledge, but they do not really open the door to the holy grail of objectivity. Phenomenology is ultimately hoisted by its own petard. It can mount a devastating critique of claims to objectivity which inevitably can be applied to and undermine its own critique.

Critical realism

This doctrine (see Bhasker, 1975) urges us to assume (though it cannot prove) that there is a real world that exists outside our minds. It is critical in suggesting that whatever we directly apprehend – people's actions and statements about these actions, for example – are not to be treated as 'what is really the case'. Another assumption is that the phenomena that we apprehend are governed by underlying structures which are said to be the equivalents of the laws of the natural sciences (also not directly observed, but required in order to explain observations). In sociology the postulated underlying structures may be structures of the human mind (as in structuralism, see pp. 103–4), relationships of production (as in Marxism), or functional prerequisites. How should we decide which of all possible structures are responsible for what we observe? The test proposed by critical realists is 'practical adequacy'. Do the explanations work? Actions whose assumptions about underlying structures are correct should have the intended consequences. Predictions based on the theory (the postulated underlying structures) should be confirmed by observations. Practical adequacy is the equivalent to what Marxists have called *praxis* (theoretically informed action). The ultimate test of a theory is said to be whether it works in practice, meaning, in Marxism, whether action by an appropriate class at an appropriate historical moment really does change the world.

Irrespective of whether they describe themselves as such, critical realism operates as the orthodox default position in contemporary sociology. Investigators assume that there is a real world, that their evidence allows them to make inferences about this real world, which usually involves invoking favoured theories to explain their findings. The problems are, first, that 'practical adequacy' is hardly a test when the theories are largely self-sealing, capable of accommodating almost any evidence, and second, observations are usually compatible with more than one set of possible underlying structures (functionalist and Marxist for example).

Triangulation

This is a way of reducing possible error. Triangulation means studying a situation using two or more different methods. The effect is said to be comparable to photographing a building from different angles, after which it is possible to make a better estimate of the overall shape of the structure. If different research methods (probably quantitative and qualitative, see below) point to the same conclusion, or if an investigator can identify a conclusion that is compatible with both sets of findings, then confidence in the conclusions is enhanced.

However, whether the same investigator or team, using different methods, but possibly with the same preconceptions loaded into each, is analogous to photographing a fixed structure from different angles, is debatable. If separate independent investigators using different methods reach the same conclusions, even this does not guarantee that the conclusions would remain robust if the situation was studied using a third, fourth and fifth method and so on. That said, triangulation is a way of strengthening truth claims.

There are no necessary links between sociologists' views on, 'What is society?' (facts or processes), positivism (emulating the natural sciences) and their choices of research methods (quantitative or qualitative). It is easy to construct stereotypes of 'hard' sociologists who are positivists and study social facts using quantitative methods, and others who adopt a processual view of society, seek to understand rather than to explain behaviour in terms of laws, and employ qualitative methods. However, there is no logical inconsistency between seeking to explain social facts (regular patterns of behaviour) through qualitative research methods, or the use of quantitative methods to explore actors' states of mind. Hence the popularity of triangulation and mixed methods research projects.

Reflexivity
Ordinary members of a society as well as sociologists can be reflexive. This means using the capacity created by human consciousness to reflect on one's circumstances, one's own abilities and desires, then select a course of action fully aware of the likely consequences and risks. In sociology reflexivity means being aware of and trying to take into account one's own preconceptions, the fragility of one's conclusions, and the limitations and sources of error that may contaminate all types of evidence.

Reflexivity is not a route to objectivity. It simply enables researchers to issue hazard warnings and to refuse to attach greater certainty to their own arguments and conclusions than their evidence warrants. Whatever position is adopted on whether sociology should try to emulate the methods of science, and whether it can establish an equivalent body of knowledge to the natural sciences, and irrespective of views on the relationship between sociology's observations and a 'real world', sociologists have no practical alternative but to work within selected paradigms which state 'what is actually known' and what needs further investigation. The stance of any active researcher is necessarily strategic naivety. Orderly research has to be within an at least partly closed system of thought, but this can be done while retaining an open mind (see Gluckman, 1964).

The techniques that sociologists can use to collect evidence are finite. Basically we can observe, ask people questions and examine objects (newspaper stories and diaries, for example) that were created for purposes other than their later use by an investigator. Sociologists who do not conduct their own primary research must rely on other investigators' observations, selections and interpretations of objects, and answers received to their questions. Irrespective of whether the procedures are deemed scientific, and irrespective of whether they are believed to give access to a real world, these are the only research techniques that sociologists can use. There are many ways of making observations, asking questions and examining objects, but a division commonly made is between the quantitative and the qualitative.

QUANTITATIVE METHODS

History

Quantitative social research, sometimes referred to rather disparagingly as fact gathering, developed in Europe during the nineteenth century. Comte was anxious to distinguish his science of society, sociology, from what he called 'social statistics'. In Europe, right up until the Second World War, sociology was the comparative study of different types of historical and contemporary societies. When social statistics (to use Comte's term) became the basis for university courses, these were called *social science* or *social administration* (what would now be called *social policy*). America was different; 'fact gathering' was part of sociology's agenda from its beginning (towards the end of the nineteenth century).

Censuses of populations had been conducted since ancient times, but during the nineteenth century the governments of modernising countries introduced regular censuses. The first of the modern censuses in Britain was conducted in 1801, the next in 1841, then every ten years except during wartime. Governments also began collecting comprehensive data about births, deaths and marriages. From time to time ad hoc enquiries collected data about health conditions, housing and especially poverty, which became a major public issue during the nineteenth century. These studies were commissioned by governments, and also by philanthropists and voluntary associations that wanted information to strengthen their campaigns for social reform, and to enable them to target their own assistance more accurately. The development of fact gathering was a response to the same social changes that stimulated the nineteenth-century theory builders. The latter wanted to understand the forces that were driving history forward. The social researchers wanted to understand some of the outcomes, especially the social problems that were being created. Both types of work claimed to be scientific. The fact gatherers were invariably in favour of reform, and usually advocated greater government intervention to improve the conditions of the people. They hoped that by scientifically demonstrating the need for reform, action and improvement would follow. They wanted to specify the sections of the population that needed various kinds of help, how many individuals and households were involved, who should be targetted, and what it would cost. The burning public issues towards the end of the nineteenth century included how many people were truly poor, in need, and how many of them were 'deserving', that is, in need through no fault of their own. The evidence from this kind of social research paved the way for the development of welfare states in twentieth-century Europe (see pp. 31–8).

Quantitative is the label given to research where the findings can be expressed in numbers: 'How many males and females, in different age groups, are in employment?' and so on. Attitudes, when measured, can be given numerical scores, with people asked to express their agreement or disagreement with statements on scales of 1–5 or 1–10, or simply to reply yes/no/don't know/no answer.

Since the nineteenth century, and during its absorption into sociology (since 1945 in Europe), the volume of quantitative research has grown dramatically. This has been made possible by advances in quantitative techniques and technology. First, there have been quantum leaps in researchers' ability to handle large volumes of data. In the nineteenth century everything had to be done by hand and brain. The findings from surveys, including censuses, had to be entered in 'ledgers' and columns of figures had to be totalled. Data from pages (possibly representing particular streets) were aggregated, then totalled into wards, then towns and cities, then regions and then grand totals for the entire country could be produced. This was laborious, time consuming and required a great deal of clerical labour. Things improved with the advent of punch cards and the card sorter. Successive columns on cardboard cards were punched to indicate whether a respondent was male or female, in which age group and so on, then the machine would sort and count the cards. The operation could be repeated to discover the proportions of males and females in different age groups who were in employment and so forth. This was much faster and permitted more complicated kinds of analysis, and simply more analysis, than was possible when working from paper by hand and brain, even though cards frequently became crumpled, causing the card sorter to seize up. Also, at the same time (1880s–1940s) mechanical calculating machines became available which could add, subtract, multiply and divide, and thereby work out percentages. This was during the age when offices were being mechanised.

The next quantum leap was with computers – originally (1940s onwards) large 'mainframe' machines. Data was recorded electronically on tape, entered into the computer, and then calculations could be completed within seconds. Since the 1960s computers have become smaller and more powerful. Every researcher has one in his or her office and probably another at home, or more likely a transportable device in which work can be carried and performed anywhere and at any time. Computer programs suitable for handling survey data have been developed. The most commonly used is the Statistical Package for the Social Sciences (SPSS). Present-day computing has multiplied the amount of analysis that can be accomplished within a finite period of time. Much can be accomplished within a single day. This, combined with the Internet which enables researchers to access data-sets in remote locations, has led to a huge expansion in quantitative research. Every year more data is collected, more analysis is accomplished, and more is written-up.

There have been parallel advances in statistics suitable for analysing survey data. Probably the most important advance has been sampling theory. In the nineteenth century it was believed that to produce findings that were valid for a large population it was necessary to survey everyone. When Seebohm Rowntree studied poverty in York in the 1890s he attempted to gather information about every working-class household in the city. Charles Booth's survey in London in the 1890s involved assessing the conditions of residents in every street in working-class districts in that city. This was subsequently shown to have been unnecessary. It was demonstrated in the early-twentieth century that the results from a representative sample would be valid for the population from which the sample was drawn within known confidence limits: for example, 99 per cent certainty that a result for the entire population would be plus or minus 2 per cent of the finding from a sample. The ability to produce useful findings about large populations from relatively small samples has increased the number of quantitative investigations that are undertaken.

There have also been massive strides in techniques of analysing data; usually ways of measuring the character and strength of relationships between variables.

- Chi square, T-tests, ANOVA (analysis of variance) and MANOVA (multiple analysis of variance) enable analysts to estimate the likelihood of differences between two or more sets of distributions (such as employment rates for males and females in different age groups) having arisen by chance within a sample.

- Correlations measure the strength of association between two variables.
- Regression and multiple regression measure the contributions of 'independent' factors to variations in a dependent variable (the contributions of gender, ethnicity and social class to differences in educational attainments, for example).
- Factor analysis assesses whether variations in a number of measurements are likely to be due to a smaller number of underlying (but unobserved) factors.
- Cluster analysis groups cases (usually individuals or households) according to how similar they are on a number of selected measurements (what kinds of tastes in music, clothing, food and beverages tend to go together, for example).

All the above, and further kinds of analysis, can be conducted by activating the necessary computer software and answers will be delivered in seconds.

Quantitative research has become a specialist field within the social sciences: sociology does not have a monopoly. Some sociologists who develop the relevant kinds of expertise (sampling, questionnaire design and data analysis) specialise in this kind of research. However, this does not necessarily mean that they are against other kinds of investigation. Sociologists differ among themselves in what they are best at, but whatever their expertise, they are most likely to favour triangulation and to treat different research methods as complementary.

Quantitative evidence can be collected from observations and by examining objects, but the most common way is by asking questions in a sample survey.

Sample Surveys

Surveys are nearly always of samples rather than censuses where an entire population is studied. There are different types of samples: probability (where there is a known probability of each case being selected) and non-probability. Quantitative surveys are usually based on probability samples. Here the aim is that the sample should be representative of the relevant population (all students at a university, over-16 year olds in a city or all rail users, for example).

The simplest kind of probability sample is the simple random sample. Here every member of a population has an equal chance of being selected. Picking every nth name on a list is not strictly random because names near to the top of the list that are not selected become unavailable for selection. This method results in a quasi-random sample (usually as near to random as matters). Pure randomness can be achieved by picking names or numbers from a hat, but nowadays it is more convenient to allow a computer to generate random numbers.

A random sample may be multistage or stratified with, for example, first of all geographical areas being selected, then persons or households within the selected areas. An investigator may use a variable sampling fraction, over-representing certain types of areas, maybe rural areas, so as to achieve adequate numbers. In this case the raw results of the survey will need to be weighted so as to obtain outcomes that are representative of the whole population. Multi-ethnic areas are often over-represented in surveys in order to obtain adequate numbers from specific ethnic minorities.

In order to select a random sample it is necessary to have a sampling frame – a list of all the persons or households who are eligible for selection. Electoral registers may be used. A university may be willing, if requested, to supply the names and addresses of all its students. A firm may be willing to do the same for all its employees. In other cases there may be no sampling frame available: everyone who has Internet access at home, everyone aged between 16 and 30 in a particular area, for example. Sometimes such samples can be selected from within larger samples of the entire populations in the relevant areas. Sometimes it is cost effective to sample a larger population and to sift out those not needed in the initial questions (those who are not on the Internet at home, for instance). Otherwise an alternative is to sample by quota.

Quotas are set by any known characteristics of the relevant population (sex, age and social class distributions, for example). Fieldworkers then have to obtain stipulated numbers of respondents to fill different 'cells'. Quota methods may be preferred even when a random sample could be selected. Quota sampling is usually less expensive than random sampling where it is necessary to locate specific individuals or addresses and call back when someone is not present or otherwise not available, or to resend questionnaires to persons who fail to reply. Non-response is a problem whatever sampling method is used. It is sometimes possible to assess whether non-response is biasing a survey if certain characteristics of the population are known in advance, in which case the findings can be weighted if a particular age or ethnic group is over- or under-represented. Quotas should guarantee that all such groups are adequately represented, but respondents will always be biased towards people who are willing to take part and available, on the streets or at home, when the fieldwork is in process. All survey organisations constantly work on their sampling methods (random or quota) and like to be able to assure clients that their achieved samples are genuinely representative. For this reason, and because they maintain teams of ready-trained fieldworkers, sociologists are most likely to contract out quantitative survey work to a specialist survey organisation.

'The more the better' is never the golden rule in determining sample size. First, an investigator must decide how accurate the results need to be. The larger a sample, the narrower the confidence interval, the spread around an achieved result within which the researcher can be 95 per cent or 99 per cent certain that the finding holds for the wider population. The investigator must anticipate the subgroups within a sample that will be examined separately during the analysis of the data. For example, a total sample of 600 should include around 300 men and 300 women, each of which may be divided into three age groups with around 100 in each. If these groups are to be disaggregated further – by region and/or social class for example – the numbers in specific subgroups will become even smaller. As a rule of thumb, 30 is generally considered the minimum number that can be used in quantitative research. A considerably larger number than 30 will usually be required to achieve the desired accuracy. Research projects always have finite budgets, but it is always unwise to opt for a sample that is larger than strictly necessary. The resources that remain can be used to enlarge a questionnaire or to allow more analysis to be undertaken.

A survey may use self-completion questionnaires or interviews. Self-completion questionnaires may be sent by mail, delivered in person, or by email with a hyperlink. Questionnaires need to be accompanied by stamped addressed envelopes if respondents are expected to return them. Personal visits to distribute and collect questionnaires can improve response rates, but if a fieldworker is to visit it will usually be sensible to conduct a survey by interview. There may be some questions where answers are most likely to be given and truthful in an anonymous questionnaire rather than face-to-face (sexual behaviour, offences committed, for instance). Respondents are always guaranteed anonymity, but they may still be invited to enter email addresses, sometimes home addresses or at least postcodes and sometimes telephone numbers. This may be so that respondents can be recontacted for a follow-up survey. However, market research firms may also add the information from a new survey to databases that are used for credit checks and to target mail shots to persons judged likely to buy a good or service. Sociologists always guarantee and preserve total anonymity and do not pass on information, but members of the public are unlikely to distinguish between different kinds of surveys. Present-day marketing practices include starting off with a few survey questions before respondents realise that this is leading to a hard or soft sell. Charities may introduce requests for donations at the end of a 'survey'. The public is being given an increasingly long list of reasons why guarantees of anonymity and 'purely for research purposes' may not be trusted. Response rates to self-completion questionnaires are low, almost always under 50 per cent and well under 10 per cent for surveys initiated by email. Questionnaires have to be kept short otherwise respondents give up. Questions must be straightforward, comprehensible by the less literate members of the public. The consensus among sociologists is that interviews yield far higher quality results. The drawback is expense: human labour is involved.

Interviews were once always face-to-face, but as the telephone has become near universal, telephone interviews have become common. This is cheaper than face-to-face, especially when there is an initial non-response and call-backs are necessary. The problem with telephone interviews is that it is easier to put down a receiver and refuse or terminate an interview midway through than to do this 'in person'. Telephone interviews usually need to be short, like questionnaires, and it can be difficult to persuade people that the initial telephone call is not another sales pitch.

Face-to-face may be in a public place (a street, town centre or visitor site). These approaches will work only with quota sampling, and the interviews must be short: there is a limit to how long passers-by can be delayed. Home interviews can be by cold calling or pre-arranged, in which case it is usual to offer alternative locations (the researcher's office, or elsewhere if the respondent so chooses), but there is no guarantee that appointments will be kept.

The main advantages of interviews include the relatively high response rates compared with self-completion questionnaires. Also, those that are pre-arranged may last an hour or longer, so more information can be collected. The interviewer can explain questions if required, and guide a respondent through complicated sets of filters (if 'no' go straight to question 23, for example). Face-to-face interviewers can collect qualitative (see below) as well as quantitative evidence. This is sociology's favourite way of asking questions.

Nowadays interviews are often computer aided, which means that the interviewer carries a laptop where the interview schedule is stored electronically, and enters answers as they are given. The software will guide the interviewer through filters and signal if questions are missed. These aids can also be used in self-completion online questionnaires. In both cases responses can be fed immediately into a database and analysis can commence as soon as interviewing is complete. This avoids the time and expense of transferring answers initially recorded on paper into an electronic data-set.

Questionnaires and interview schedules may be fully structured, which means that the questions and possible answers are laid-out for the respondent. An unstructured instrument would be used only in qualitative research: this consists of a list of topics to which a person is expected to respond. These instruments are normally used only in interviews, where the interviewer can follow initial remarks with further prompts. A partly structured instrument has pre-set questions which may be followed by a combination of pre-set answers and spaces for free response. Unstructured answers may be analysed qualitatively (see below), or coded immediately into categories for entry into a quantitative data-set.

Observation

This can be done quantitatively. For example, school classrooms may be observed, noting occasions when the teacher addresses the entire class, the occasions when a pupil initiates an interaction with the teacher, plus pupil–pupil interaction. Provided some details about the pupils are known and recorded, it becomes possible to observe whether boys and girls, and pupils from different ethnic groups, behave and are treated differently. If observations are made in more than one classroom, it becomes possible to compare the classroom management of different teachers. If enough classrooms are studied, comparisons can be made according to the ages, sex and ethnicity of the teachers. What people say may differ from what they actually do. Hence the unique value of observation.

Players' performances during sports events can be quantified. This may be from a recording or during live play. It is possible, in a soccer match, to measure the distances that individual players cover, the number of passes they make, the proportion of passes that are successful and so on.

Observation has strengths, and also limitations. It is impossible to observe subjective states, but these may be related to behaviour in a multi-methods project.

Objects

The objects that are quantified are usually texts: newspaper stories for example. Various aspects of content can be quantified:

- Topics: such as the number of stories about education.
- Themes, the issues: pupil behavior, social mobility, standards of attainment.
- Discourses, how issues are discussed. Are pupils fulfilling their potential? Are they being prepared for their future work roles?
- The frame, the wider context in which the issue is located: national

decline in standards of behaviour, the effects of government policies.

It becomes possible to compare how the same news is covered in different newspapers, and also to track changes over time in how education is reported in the press.

The Internet is proving a valuable source of texts, especially interactive sites where members of an online community discuss an issue, or blogs where individuals present themselves. There are hazards. Which larger populations do site visitors represent? Are their virtual selves the same as their real selves? Despite these uncertainties, texts are valuable because there is no possibility of an observer effect, often called a Hawthorne effect in sociology. This name is taken from the site of a company, a district of Chicago (USA), where researchers in the 1920s were investigating the effects of varying the illumination, and the frequency and length of breaks, but eventually concluded that the changes in worker behaviour that were recorded were due primarily to their knowledge that they were being observed. There are always possible observer effects during live observation, in interviews, and even with self-completion questionnaires where people may answer according to their perceptions and views about the persons or organisation responsible for the survey. People may not always tell the truth about their behaviour or reveal what they really think. Objects, including texts, are completely free from possible observer effects; hence their unique value.

Assessment

Quantitative research yields what may appear to be hard facts, resembling Durkheim's social facts which have been plucked from the real world through systematic observation, asking questions and examining objects. Sociologists all realise that the investigator always and necessarily plays a role in constructing these facts; they are made rather than simply discovered and unearthed. Respondents can answer only the questions that they are asked, and the researcher decides the questions. The researcher decides which issues, ideas (hypotheses) to examine. The researcher decides who to ask. The analyst of texts decides which topics, themes, types of discourse and which frames to look for. Quantitative research can achieve high levels of *reliability*. This is a technical term which means that the same findings would be achieved if the methods were repeated by a second investigator. Reliability does not guarantee *validity*, another technical term meaning that the instrument (interview schedule, observation matrix and so on) measures exactly what it claims to measure.

Quantitative research does not yield objective, mind-free knowledge. Its merit is that it is possible to examine large numbers of cases which are representative of even larger populations. This applies to observations and texts as well as questionnaire and interview surveys. The use of statistical techniques enables relationships between 'variables' to be identified. These relationships need to be explained. The variables may be measurements of behaviour or subjective states (identities, attitudes, values and views of the world). Although the researcher always plays a part in the construction of these variables, there can be a reasonable assumption that external reality also contributes.

Causality is always attributed. It can never be observed. Quantitative research is good at measuring the relationships between whatever is measured, but less effective at uncovering the processes that are responsible for the relationships. Qualitative research (see below) has the edge here. Quantitative research has the edge in testing hypotheses. The investigator has to design research instruments in advance: it is impossible to proceed without some preconceptions of the likely findings.

It is sometimes claimed that qualitative research is best at generating new insights – hypotheses (grounded theories) – that may then need to be examined in quantitative enquiries. This is not always true. Once collected, quantitative data can usually be analysed in ways that were not planned in advance. Unexpected relationships between variables can be revealed. Investigators are then required to rethink their original ideas, to entertain new hypotheses, which may then be further explored in data already at hand, or may require another, follow-up investigation.

QUALITATIVE RESEARCH

'Minimally structured' would be a better label. The aim is always to allow the subjects to guide the collection of information and its interpretation. This kind of relationship between a researcher and the subjects is called *iterative*. Observations are made without an observer-imposed matrix. The aim is to allow the actors to show not only what is happening but what is important. The subjects in a project are allowed to explain the significance of objects – their collections of photographs or music, for example. Texts, including interview transcripts, are read through more than once before deciding which themes, discourses and frames should be noted.

Qualitative evidence is sometimes called 'soft' in contrast to the 'hard facts' produced in quantitative research, yet conducting minimally structured research is anything but a soft option. It is extremely demanding and difficult. Successful practitioners find it hard to explain how to do it. There are no equivalents to the manuals on how to select a sample, to design a questionnaire and analyse a quantitative data-set. This is because qualitative research always needs to be fine-tuned to the situations and groups that are studied. There can be no standard template. Even so, qualitative research can be just as rigorous and systematic as any other kind of investigation. The methods are not especially subjective, though they may lack the reliability (see above, p. 124) of quantitative methods. Qualitative research is risky. If a fieldworker leaves a project then much of the evidence is lost. Also, it is difficult for beginners to demonstrate the competence that would convince a funding body. Yet the findings probably have greater claims to validity – presenting to a wider audience an authoritative account of what is really happening in the groups and situations that are studied – and are no less trustworthy than other kinds of evidence. The situations, groups and individuals who are studied are never large in number, and can never be guaranteed to be representative of larger populations. This kind of research does not try to answer 'How many?' questions. Its strengths are in revealing how particular actors perceive and feel about their situations and themselves, thereby identifying the processes that are necessary parts of causal explanations in sociology.

Ethnography

This means studying people in their normal environments. Simply conducting unstructured interviews (see below) is not ethnography, which is sometimes called the anthropological method. Social anthropologists (as they are called in Europe) or cultural anthropologists (the American term) have traditionally spent extended periods among the people being studied, first learning the language, 'living in the village', sharing the villagers' lives while interfering as little as possible. Ethnography combines observation, taking opportunities to ask people questions about their behaviour and beliefs, and to explain the significance of objects that are part of their lives. A golden rule in all qualitative research is to continue until nothing new is being learnt. This is a formidable challenge. After a few weeks in a community an anthropologist might feel that he or she is beginning to understand the way of life. After six months the researcher will probably have realised that some earlier impressions were plain wrong. After two years the investigator may well have drawn similar conclusions about much of what he or she knew after six months. Qualitative research is time-demanding, and there is no way in which a fieldworker can hand over to a colleague. This kind of fieldwork is definitely not a soft option.

The core method in ethnography is always participant observation. The researcher must become a participant in the group that is being studied. In this way the researcher will not only learn about but experience the people's lives. He or she should not merely gain access to but share and feel their views of the world. There are two ways in which participant observation can come about. Sometimes a participant also becomes an observer, which occurs when someone who trains in sociology returns to and studies a group, usually a group with which he or she has retained a bond. This is probably the only way of conducting a participant observer study in a criminal gang or among hard drug users, but many sociologists have used their backgrounds in lower class communities, working-class occupations, sport and music cultures to go back or use their ongoing associations to do research and produce sociological accounts. Alternatively, an observer may become a participant in a previously alien group and culture – the route always taken by the original anthropologists. In these cases the researcher needs to become accepted as a participant and may be unsuccessful. The researcher needs to be accepted to the extent that he or she can share the way of life of the group and gain access to its members' views of the world, their concerns and hopes. Needless to say, a researcher can never become exactly like ordinary participants. Any participant who becomes a researcher will be atypical of the group. An observer who went completely native would never emerge to write an account for sociology.

Nowadays it is difficult to build a long-term career as an active ethnographer, though there are exceptions such as Michael Burawoy, the American sociologist who was elected President of the International Sociological Association in 2010 (see Chapter 8). Social anthropologists used to perform their initial extended fieldwork as postgraduates and then make refresher visits to the societies that they had studied throughout their careers. This will not work in modern societies because neighbourhoods, workplaces and occupations change too rapidly. There are still many postgraduate ethnographers in sociology, but when it becomes necessary to combine research with teaching and administration, most switch to other kinds of qualitative research.

Unstructured Interviews

Here the interviewer raises issues or topics, and encourages a respondent to talk freely. The interviewer has to avoid 'leading' the respondent. Short answers can be followed by requests to amplify. 'Why do you say that?' is a good question. 'Would you say that . . .?' is leading, putting words or ideas into a respondent's head.

In ethnography it may be an advantage for a researcher to be similar to the subjects in background, gender, ethnicity and age, though this was never the case in early social anthropology. Fieldworkers have to gain acceptance, and this will be easy or difficult depending on the relationship between the researcher's and the subjects' social and cultural locations, plus personality factors will also play a part. An academic sociologist is unlikely to be embraced by a criminal gang. A male investigator will find it difficult to conduct ethnography in a women's caucus. However, with unstructured interviews it can be an advantage if the researcher is from outside the subject's culture. This enables the fieldworker to request clarification of points that an insider would be expected to understand.

Unstructured interviews are usually tape-recorded unless a respondent objects. Answers have to be recorded verbatim, not translated into the researcher's everyday or sociological terms. An interviewer will probably take notes even during a tape-recording: smiles and frowns cannot be taped. The transcripts from a series of interviews will be read and reread, identifying themes, discourses and frames, which will then be used to code passages of text. There is software, like *NVivo*, which can assist. When the results of the research are written-up the respondents' own words will be used as much as possible. The subjects have to be given voice. What respondents have actually said has to be separated from any interpretations made by the researcher.

Focus Groups

These were pioneered by market researchers and political opinion pollsters to complement interview surveys. The standard procedure is to bring together a group, usually with between eight and 12 members who are similar in what are believed to be significant ways – parents of young children, employees who are approaching retirement, undecided voters – depending on the topic to be explored. A facilitator presents stimulus material. This may be a proposed advert: 'Does this make you more likely to buy . . .?' It may be a photograph of a politician or a policy statement: 'How does this make you feel?' Sociologists use focus groups in basically the same way.

As with unstructured interviews, focus groups may be stand alone or they may precede or follow a larger survey. If the latter, the aim will be to discover what people meant when they replied that they hated X or agreed with Y. If the interviews or focus groups precede a larger survey, the aim will be to help to design appropriate questions.

As with unstructured interviews, in a focus group the investigator should facilitate, draw out, but not suggest views. The purpose of the group situation is to provoke discussion, which will prompt participants to say what they really feel, to discover whether there is an underlying consensus or a basic division of opinion on a topic. The proceedings are always recorded, preferably video-recorded. Ideally, someone other than the facilitator will be in charge of these arrangements. If the tape is purely audio, someone has to note who is speaking. Participants are invariably offered expenses and a gift (a shop voucher or book token) for their time and trouble. The same inducements may be offered when people attend pre-arranged interviews away from their own homes or offices, and sometimes when they are interviewed at home. The rewards are never so attractive that participants may wish to perform well and give the 'right' answers so that they will be invited back.

Narrative Interviews

In these interviews each respondent tells a story. This might be about their involvement and experiences in a particular situation or event – a strike or political demonstration, for example. However, the story is usually about their own lives, probably focusing on a particular aspect – career in education, the labour market, or family and housing histories. These interviews will usually start by noting key dates, depending on the aspect of the respondent's life that is to be the focus: dates of birth, leaving education, job changes, marriage(s), moving address, birth dates of children and so on. These key dates will then be used as milestones in the narrative.

Sociologists know that personal biographies, like history, are always created in the present. History is constantly rewritten as we learn more about the past, but also for what it can tell us about how we arrived at the present. People make sense of their lives, develop coherent narratives, in the light of where their lives have led up to the present moment in time. People cannot have known at the time whether a redundancy would scar them for life or act as a challenge after which their careers flourished. They will speak differently about a past event depending on what has happened since. The aim of these interviews, therefore, is to better understand how people have reached their current situations, but equally to understand how they are projecting and planning their lives into the future, and how their current views about themselves and their social environment have been shaped. As in all qualitative research, these interviews are usually tape-recorded (with permission), and the transcripts will be read and reread.

Sampling

Qualitative research is necessarily small-scale – too small to make it useful to select a probability sample. Respondents are usually selected purposively – couples in ethnically mixed marriages, lower class students at elite universities, or transsexuals, for example. People may be selected because they are known and available. This is called a convenience sample. 'Snowballing' may be used, where one respondent suggests others who should be suitable.

Samples do not need to be representative, given the typical aims of qualitative research. A researcher may already know that A is related to B. The purpose of a qualitative study will be to discover 'how' and 'why'. If an aim is to generate theory – to suggest explanations – representativeness is irrelevant. As Karl Popper insisted (see pp. 110–111), there are no set procedures for conjecturing good or bad hypotheses, which may subsequently be tested with representative samples.

In qualitative research there is no preferred sample size. The golden rule is that the researcher should continue until the evidence becomes repetitive and nothing new is being learnt. This may be after 10, 20, 30 or more interviews. At this point, never before, the quantity is 'enough'.

PROGRESS IN QUALITATIVE AND QUANTITATIVE METHODS

It is not an exaggeration to say that sociology has a love affair with its qualitative studies. The books can be a 'good read'. They encourage students who are most likely to decide to be qualitative in their own research projects. The books and articles speak about real lives. The findings feel authentic. They uncover causal links between people's past experiences, states of mind and present actions. A problem is that these research methods have not discovered ways of overcoming their limitations. As noted above, the studies are small-scale. They are difficult to replicate and thereby demonstrate reliability. Persuasive writing makes the findings feel valid, but it is difficult to corroborate this in independent investigations.

Quantitative research has made giant quantum leaps during the last 30 years, partly through advances in statistical techniques, but mainly through the ability to create and maintain large data-sets, to harmonise (render comparable) different data-sets, and make these resources available to the global research community. These resources now include the following.

- Birth cohort studies, in which panels of individuals are followed-up from birth throughout their entire lifetimes. This enables the long-term consequences of early experiences to be tracked. Sequential cohort studies enable changes over time in the life course to be identified. In Britain there are five ongoing birth cohort studies of persons born in 1946, 1958, 1970, 2000 and 2012.

- Household panel studies in which all members of households are studied on successive occasions. The *British Household Panel Study* (BHPS) commenced in 1991 based on around 10 500 adults in 5500 households. This panel has now been absorbed into a larger *Understanding Society* panel study, based on 40 000 households containing around 100 000 individuals, who were first interviewed in 2009–10 and will be followed-up indefinitely. Since the mid-1990s the BHPS has been part of a *European Household Panel Survey* in which comparable data is assembled from 15 participating countries.
- Time use studies, in which people record their activities throughout typical days, have been conducted occasionally in Britain since the 1960s. The results of all these surveys, and around 60 comparable data-sets from 22 other countries, have been harmonised and are available through the Centre for Time Use Research at Oxford University. The *European Time Use Survey* gathers harmonised data from 10 European countries.
- Victim surveys are now regarded as the most accurate way of measuring crime. Representative samples are asked about their experiences as victims. The *British Crime Survey* was first conducted in 1982, was repeated bi-annually until 2000 and is now an annual survey.
- The *Active People Survey*: since 2005 this bi-annual survey has collected data about participation in sports and cultural activities from large (around 150 000) representative samples of the population of England.
- EUROSTAT is the European Union's data bank which contains harmonised data on numerous aspects of economic (and other parts of) life in all member countries. The Organisation for Economic Cooperation and Development, and the United Nations and its affiliates, maintain similar 'banks' with harmonised data from large numbers of countries.

The reason for the extremely large samples in some of the above surveys is that researchers and their funding bodies have talked to potential users of the findings, mainly government departments. They have turned-out to want representative results for substate territories (local authority areas), and for specific sections of the populations (families with disabled children, people who have claimed incapacity benefits and so on). Smaller numbers would be adequate for pure social science purposes. Large-scale quantitative surveys have grown even larger because this actually makes them better value per unit of spending for the wider society (or certain groups therein).

The above developments have transformed the working lives of quantitative researchers. They may still design, conduct, analyse then write-up their own self-contained projects, but the funds available for research are increasingly channelled into building and maintaining the data-sets listed above. Hence quantitative researchers are increasingly involved in the design and content of 'common good' projects, and draw on these resources. They need to specialise on particular data-sets. They need to keep up-to-date on the variables that these data-sets contain, and on previous and concurrent work that is being undertaken on the data. Becoming a proficient user of these data resources is time consuming. The data-sets contain thousands of variables. Analysts need to create and constantly update their own files of variables on which they base their own work.

In comparison, qualitative research remains in a time-warp. Software to assist in the analysis of texts has been developed and is now widely used. There are archives in which qualitative resources (interview transcripts, photographs and fieldnotes) can be deposited. These archives are used. For example, Mike Savage (2010) has used archived material from social surveys of the 1950s and 1960s in a study of how social science and British society were changing at that time. However, this kind of foray is occasional in contrast to the now routine use of data banks. Qualitative evidence deteriorates in value when separated from those who conducted the relevant fieldwork. It is difficult to standardise and replicate qualitative studies, so cross-national comparative research is rare. Karen Evans and Walter Heinz's (1994) comparative study of young people in Germany and England has been a rare exception. Working internationally, qualitatively and comparatively, requires the same fieldworkers to be able to work in all the countries that are involved. This requires language skills as well as considerable amounts of research time and money.

It is also difficult to conduct extended longitudinal qualitative studies. Sheila Henderson and colleagues (2007) tracked the lives of 100 young people in five different UK locations from 1996 to 2006. This project partly overlapped the *Timescapes Project* which tracked 400 young people who were initially aged 6–13 in 2003 until 2009 when they were aged 12–19 (Edwards and Weller, 2010). The volume of evidence that projects such as these amass is formidable: hundreds of pages of interview transcripts. Subsamples have usually been extracted for detailed analysis. This is despite the projects being only modestly longitudinal compared with, for example, the *British Household Panel Survey* and the birth cohort studies.

It is impossible to conduct ethnography in a modern society in the manner of the social anthropologists who would live in a village, learn all about its way of life and return periodically for updates. Modern societies change more rapidly. Lives move on. People move out of homes and neighbourhoods. There is some loss of value every time qualitative evidence (interview transcripts and fieldnotes) are passed on to researchers in different locations, and as research staff leave and join a longitudinal project. A more basic problem is that while the anthropological method can be adopted by sociologists who study modern societies, it is impossible to conduct a qualitative study of a whole way of modern life.

HOW IS SOCIOLOGICAL RESEARCH DISTINCTIVE?

Ethics

Sociologists can claim that their knowledge is acquired more systematically and more critically than the everyday. They can claim that, unlike journalists, they are more interested in the general than the particular. Nowadays they are also likely to be able to say that their research had prior ethical approval.

In many countries procedures have been introduced to assure the public that sociological research complies with ethical standards. Some sociologists feel that these procedures are an expensive cure (in researcher time) for a non-existent problem. Nevertheless, many sociological associations have adopted codes of ethics. In theory, members could be disciplined and expelled for breaches, but there are no known cases of this. The guidelines enable sociologists to project the public appearance of a proper profession.

Universities and research organisations in many countries have rules that require the approval of ethics committees prior to undertaking any research that involves human subjects. This 'medical model', often extended to non-human animals nowadays, is applied to any research that involves observing or questioning people, which encompasses most sociological projects including those undertaken by students. Universities are protecting themselves from possible legal action. They wish to be able to claim that they have taken all reasonable precautions if anyone should claim (there have been no known cases) of being damaged or otherwise mistreated during sociological research. Schools may require parental consent forms to be signed and returned before pupils can be asked to complete questionnaires in class.

Ethical guidelines require sociologists to observe two main principles. First, that their research should not harm the subjects. This is unlikely during the research process, but it is impossible to guarantee, and some researchers might be delighted if particular kinds of businesses, political movements or gangs suffered harm following the publication of the research. These risks may be reduced by guaranteeing anonymity and confidentiality, but case studies lose much of the fine detail that makes them interesting if the researchers have to disguise the particular towns, industries, sites and groups that have been investigated. Also, such anonymity makes replication impossible.

The second principle is that the subjects in a project should take part under conditions of informed consent. This means that they should be told about the character and purposes of the research, and made aware that they can refuse to take part or withdraw at any time. Subjects are sometimes asked to sign consent forms indicating that all this is understood. If applied rigidly, these guidelines would prohibit all unobtrusive and undisclosed observation, including forms of participant observation where the observer becomes a participant without the group being made aware of the individual's intentions. The guideline would make it difficult to research certain kinds of political and religious movements, and deviant subcultures. It would also impede participants becoming observers. Fortunately, ethics committees can exercise discretion.

CONCLUSIONS

Sociology does not have a special research *methods* problem. The ways in which sociologists collect evidence are straightforward: look (observe objects, situations and actors) and ask, which can all be done in structured or unstructured ways. These methods cannot be extended, and none of them are used only in sociology. Ethnography was pioneered in social anthropology. Surveys are used in all social sciences. Any weaknesses in sociology's methods cannot be weaknesses in sociology alone. Sociology is different from some cognate disciplines in that there is no method in which it has monopoly expertise as do economists with econometrics (the analysis of economic data) and psychologists with their banks of tests for measuring different attitudes, personality traits and other states of mind including personal well-being.

Sociology does have distinctive *methodological* problems. Methodology is the study of methods. All disciplines need to constantly examine and try to improve their methods. There are always disagreements, but in sociology these are especially fierce and deep. Sociologists have been unable to agree on whether the knowledge that they can produce is similar to or basically different from the knowledge of the natural sciences on the one side, and everyday common sense on the other. Sociologists cannot agree on whether mind-free (objective) knowledge of the social is possible, whether their various methods are exposing the forces that really govern societies, or even about the basic elements of the social.

Thomas Kuhn (see pp. 111–12) noted that at any time the natural sciences have possessed generally accepted paradigms. Anyone who refuses to accept the paradigm is pushed to the fringe until points are reached when the evidence produced by research within a paradigm requires an overhaul of the paradigm itself, in which case scientists formerly dismissed as mad may become the new geniuses. Other social sciences avoid methodological disputes by limiting their ambitions. Mainstream economics operates with an economic model of man which claims no more than to identify certain processes within how actual economies work. Remarkably, economists have been able to persuade many of the world's governments to try to make their countries' economies work like their model. Sociology does not have an equivalent agreed model of society, so has no chance of achieving the influence of economics. Mainstream social psychology studies the circumstances that foster particular states of mind including well-being and ill-being, the types of action most likely to be taken in given situations by actors who possess particular states of mind (personality traits), and devises measurements that predict who will perform best in given occupations, on educational programmes, respond to ways of treating offenders and so forth. They do not try to incorporate the ideas of Freud (pp. 92–4), Mead (pp. 93–4) or symbolic interactionism (pp. 99–102). Political scientists, educational researchers and students of sport and culture are mostly content to describe how their 'subsystems' work. Sociology has methodological problems because the discipline remains incredibly ambitious. It seeks theories that apply to all aspects of all societies, and which will explain the course of history including recent transformations. Sociology aspires to become part of history itself, maybe by replacing religions (see Chapter 8), inspiring social movements, and producing evidence that leads to reform and improvement in people's lives. These are the features that make sociology exceptionally challenging and interesting. The problem is that sociologists are unable to reach agreed answers and this forces them to inspect and criticise each other's methods.

The practice of sociology has other features that make it different from any other social science. Unlike economists, sociologists are never at ease when using official, government statistics. Sociologists do not trust this evidence. They always prefer to collect (or create) their own. Unlike social psychologists, sociologists rarely replicate each other's projects. Sociologists rarely use entire batches of questions that have been used (and deemed validated) in previous enquiries. Every group and situation that is studied seems somehow different in ways that demand tailor-made instruments. None of its research methods are exclusive to sociology, but sociology is different in having such a wide range of methods at its disposal. These characteristics of sociology are responses to its core subject matter – social transformations and divisions. The subject matter requires sociology to be intellectually ambitious, responsive to changes and flexible in its selection of appropriate methods.

8.   The role of sociology in society

INTRODUCTION

Sociology cannot avoid being part of its own subject matter. It is close to unique in this respect. All academic disciplines are parts of their host societies which create jobs, pay salaries, provide research funds, supply students then employ graduates. The knowledge developed and taught in all disciplines is used in some way or another. The natural sciences and the related technologies have applications. So do the human and social sciences such as psychology and economics, and so does sociology. Apparently useless subjects such as classics may play important roles in reproducing sociocultural elites. However, no other subject except philosophy needs to apply its own disciplinary gaze to itself. This is a way in which sociology is different. Sociology studies whole societies. Sociology, along with all other academic disciplines, is part of these societies. Thus sociologists are professionally required to examine themselves and their work. In doing so sociologists inevitably consider the extent to which they can set the terms of their wider social engagement.

Most sociologists, at some stage in their careers, have always aspired to make a difference. It is true that some seek knowledge for its own sake. Some students just want the qualification. However, most researchers and writers would prefer someone outside their discipline to read their output, heed their ideas, and use their findings and theories. Most sociology students hope that their better understanding of society will somehow help them to make their societies better places. In these respects nothing has changed since the birth of sociology. The nineteenth-century theory-builders wanted to identify laws of history and thereby speed and ease the birth of more advanced social orders. The fact gatherers hoped that the sheer weight of their evidence would lead to improvements in social conditions. Sociologists' aspirations have not changed, but today they face new challenges. One is reaching any audience beyond sociology. Most sociologists have always wanted to develop a public discipline, accessible beyond its teachers, researchers and students. Nowadays a concern is that no one else is listening. This is despite there being more sociologists than ever before. Collectively we may have more voice. Our output commands more library space. There are lots of downloads of the more popular papers, but downloading is different than reading, which is different than understanding, which is different than doing something with the knowledge. Sociology's problem is not unique to the discipline. The public intellectual is a threatened species. The space once occupied by academic experts is now contested by TV and press journalists, and the think tanks attached to political parties. Another change is that sociologists today lack the confidence of their nineteenth-century predecessors that they possess superior insights that give them the right to instruct people on how they ought to live, and to define for governments the good societies that they should try to create. Meanwhile, it has become easier than ever before for sociologists to become 'servants of power', conducting research that will assist governments and businesses to pursue their objectives. The output from this research may have huge 'impact' while attracting few readers outside the government departments that sponsor the studies. The following sections explain how this has created divisions among sociologists between the professionals (who research and write for other sociologists), policy sociologists (the servants of power), various kinds of self-defined critical sociologists and those who are trying to be public sociologists.

THE SCIENCE OF PROGRESS

In the nineteenth century it was not common practice to make a clear distinction between statements of fact and judgements of value; between what 'is' and what 'ought' to be. This applied in everyday life and among intellectuals. From ancient times onwards philosophers had made moral judgements. Churches had subsequently claimed ultimate moral authority. By the nineteenth century, science was winning the challenge that had begun in earlier centuries over questions of astronomy and the history of the world and its species. The social sciences were claiming to be the authoritative voices on how societies worked, and their pioneers believed that it was they who could make the authoritative judgements on how people ought to live, and how societies could and should progress.

The nineteenth-century founding fathers of sociology developed theories about long-term historical changes. They all recognised history as a process during which societies evolved from the simple to the complex, and that human thought and morals had changed in parallel. The most complex societies were treated as the most advanced along a common global evolutionary path. They had the most productive economies, the most powerful armies, the most effective forms of government, and, it was believed, superior morals. They were the most 'civilised'. This was one of the justifications for colonialism. Sociology's evolutionary theorists believed that having identified history's course, they could project history forward into an even more advanced stage, and demonstrate scientifically how progress could be accelerated and how attendant problems could be handled.

Auguste Comte did not just describe and explain how a scientific mind-set was replacing metaphysics and changing the world. He was a passionate advocate of science. He was confident that science improved people's lives, and that this was a plain matter of fact rather than just his opinion. His sociology was not intended to yield scientific evidence that others (politicians and business leaders) would put to their own uses. Comte's sociology was to tell them how they should act for their own and the wider humanity's good. Positivism was to become a new religion, and its experts (like Comte) were to become the new high priests.

Durkheim's scientific method was more rigorous, but he had very similar expectations and aspirations to Comte as regards the role of sociology. Durkheim had no doubt that the evolutionary path was delivering real progress, and his sociology was to explain how this progress could be reconciled with the maintenance of social solidarity. Durkheim's view was that all societies needed a common belief system, judgements in which everyone could have confidence and authoritative judges who were 'worshipped'. Traditional religions were relinquishing this role, and science, with sociology foremost, was expected to take their place.

In 1907 Leonard T. Hobhouse (1864–1929) became the London School of Economics' first Professor of Sociology (and the first in Britain). Hobhouse's ideas bore a close resemblance to those of Hegel and Comte. He believed that social progress was driven by the development of the human mind, thought and morals. In simple societies thoughts and actions were said to be driven by impulses. In the most advanced societies people's ideas and related actions were based on evidence and reason. Hobhouse believed that in simple societies moral obligations were felt only towards close associates, people known personally, primarily kin. Progress was said to lead to behaviour being governed by general ethical principles. Hobhouse believed that progress was leading towards a single world society which would be based on universally applied ethics (Hobhouse, 1915). Hobhouse's student, protégé and successor as Professor of Sociology at the LSE was Morris Ginsberg (1889–1970), who believed that he was developing an 'objectivist' theory of ethics in studying links between economic development, social and moral progress among twentieth-century societies (Ginsberg, 1947).

Sociologists were not alone in the confidence with which they made moral judgements. Adam Smith (1723–1790), regarded by many as the founder of modern economics, had no reservations in approving the use of self-interest to spread prosperity or in deciding which services could and could not be left to the market. Jeremy Bentham (1748–1832) and other utilitarian philosophers believed that in espousing their core principle to judge what was right and best – the greatest happiness for the greatest number – they were simply stating a matter of fact. They did not regard it as purely their own opinion that people ought to seek happiness, or that they ought to be made happy by whatever made them feel this way.

The nineteenth-century middle classes had great confidence in their ability to know what was best for others. They expected anyone who was equally well-informed to agree with them. The social fact gatherers, the pioneers of social research, believed that they had only to demonstrate the numbers of people living in hardship, short of the necessities of life, coping in over-crowded and insanitary dwellings, for it to become self-evident that those able to do so (philanthropists and governments) should take the steps needed to change these conditions. Marxists were equally confident that they knew the type of consciousness that the working class should develop and the kinds of action that should follow. They believed that they understood the historical trajectory of capitalist societies, and that in the long run history would prove them right.

During the first half of the twentieth century there was a fundamental shift in the intellectual climate, and new orthodoxies were articulated most clearly by the Vienna Circle of philosophers (see pp. 109–10). First, as explained in Chapter 7, they introduced the falsification principle into scientific discourse. Propositions had to be falsifiable yet remain intact following relevant observations if they were to be accepted. Second, the Vienna Circle insisted on a separation of 'is' and 'ought' statements, matters of fact (which could be settled on the basis of evidence) and judgements of value. They insisted that neither type of statement could be derived from the other. Science could settle disputes about facts, but had no special authority to speak on issues of value. Thus science could develop value-free knowledge, but had no privileged position for deciding the uses to which such knowledge should be put.

After 1945 European sociology began to incorporate fact gathering, survey methods and statistical techniques for analysing data. The logical positivist doctrines were in harmony with this type of sociology (see below). Mike Savage (2010) has contrasted sociology's 'technicians' of the 1950s and 1960s with its gentlemanly intellectuals of earlier years. The latter had no serious qualms when passing judgement on the behaviour of the people who they studied.

We should note here that the Vienna Circle's doctrines did not prohibit social scientists from studying their subjects' values and morals – how their subjects thought people should behave. There was no prohibition on resolving by evidence whether certain ethical principles were observed universally, or whether there was a convergence in morals as societies developed economically. Indeed, the study of values has grown into a substantial subdiscipline within sociology. The *World Values Survey*, now conducted in 180 countries, has shown how economic growth is linked to declining support for traditions and religious authority, and how post-industrial, post-scarcity conditions are linked to a decline in the importance attached to security, greater support for self-expression, and for certain types of cultural diversity (acceptance of abortion and homosexuality, for example) (see Inglehart, 1977, 1997; Welzel et al., 2003). These surveys describe and propose explanations, but abstain from making value judgements about different societies' values.

It is not philosophical arguments alone that have undermined the social sciences' confidence in their superior value judgements. The twentieth-century world wars, the Holocaust, and Stalin's regime in the Soviet Union that killed more people than the Holocaust, shattered confidence that humanity was becoming progressively more civilised. The doubts have been continuously reinforced: in the twenty-first century by the willingness of 'coalitions of the willing' to practise so-called liberal intervention in Afghanistan and Iraq and justify the slaughter of civilians as 'collateral damage'. During the second half of the twentieth century the old certainty was lost that improvements in economic standards of living automatically improved the quality of life. Also, by then it was realised that the so-called simple societies had extremely complicated kinship systems; behaviour was no more impulsive than in the rest of the world and moral rules applied in all their areas of life. Thus Morris Ginsberg ended his career (he lectured into the 1960s) as an isolated figure in UK (and global) sociology.

We can note that although sociology has stood aside, others have continued to declare or claim to detect ethical principles that should be applied everywhere. In 1948 the United Nations adopted its famous declaration of human rights that should be protected by law in all countries. These rights include freedom of movement, and prohibition of slavery and torture. All member states are supposed to subscribe to and protect these rights. In 1950 the European Council adopted a convention on human rights. It created a commission to investigate alleged infringements, and a court to decide. Countries which sign the convention (now a condition of EU membership) are required to incorporate judgements of the European Court into their own laws, and to enforce these laws in their own courts. Maybe history is vindicating Hobhouse's forecast of the development and application of universal ethical principles. Or are these examples of the world's most powerful countries trying to impose their values on others?

We can also note that the economically advanced societies continue, in international arenas, to claim the high moral ground. They decide that less developed countries ought to be developed. They decided that former Communist countries should make a transition into Western-type democracies and market economies. The world's most powerful countries (in economic and military senses) lay down rules for international trade and finance via the World Trade Organisation, the World Bank and the International Monetary Fund. NATO has acted in the former Yugoslavia and Afghanistan as if it represented the entire international community. So did the USA-led 'coalition of the willing' that invaded Iraq in 2003.

Clearly, there is not an international consensus on whether Western-type democracy is the best political system for all countries, whether men and women should have equal access to all social roles, whether all forms of sexuality are equally acceptable, whether capital punishment is ever justified, or whether freedom of expression should be extended to criticism of governments and the organisation of opposition. The most powerful countries are no less determined than in the colonial era to export their own values. This, according to Samuel Huntington (1996), is leading to a clash of civilisations, most notably between the West and Islam. Its nineteenth-century founders would have deplored how contemporary sociology has remained aloof from these twenty-first-century global justice issues: the territory has been left to politicians, and academic and practising lawyers.

VALUE-FREE SOCIOLOGY: THE RISE OF THE POLICY SOCIOLOGIST

In the decades following the Second World War, when Max Weber's work was being translated from the original German and published in other languages (mainly English), Weber was widely understood as having advocated value-free sociology. This was probably a misreading of Weber who personally was heavily involved in public affairs in Germany, especially during and following the First World War. However, Weber believed that in bureaucracies private interests could be excluded from the performance of official duties, and he also believed that science could be a vocation. German culture and the related organisation of economic life enabled nearly all occupations to be treated as vocations. They are 'professions' (a term with wider application in Germany than in its Anglo-Saxon meaning) for which individuals are trained and qualified, in which they are skilled, where they remain for long-term careers, and thereby can earn self-respect and public esteem for their professional conduct. Weber believed that science could be such a vocation in which the professionals were dedicated to extending and assisting in the application of knowledge in their fields. Individual scientists would normally have views on the uses to which the knowledge that they developed ought to be put, and the areas in which it was important to expand knowledge. This, of course, applies in every profession. Advocates of value-free sociology have never argued that individual sociologists should be value-free. This is impossible. Their values will always influence the topics that individuals choose to study and how they interpret their findings. As recognised at the beginning of this chapter, individual sociologists have usually wanted their work to make an impact in their societies. Most sociologists have always been on the political left, but in principle sociology can be allied with any position on the political spectrum. Value-freedom, if possible at all, results not from individuals somehow isolating their professional role from their private and political selves, but from a professional community, in this case a community of scientists, interrogating each other's work.

Before and following the Second World War there was a prolonged debate within and beyond sociology about the role of intellectuals and the extent, if at all, to which they could view the world independently of sectional interests. Karl Mannheim (1893–1947) contrasted the 'ideologies' that were likely to be espoused by those with vested interests in the status quo with the 'utopias', views of a better future, that were most likely to appeal to the disadvantaged. Marxists generally felt that intellectuals had to side with one group or the other. Mannheim, in contrast, believed that intellectuals could occupy a distinct position (Mannheim, 1929). Did this give intellectuals an objective view? The eventual consensus in sociology was that they could simply view the world from their own particular professional vantage point.

However, in the 1950s and 1960s an orthodox view among sociologists was that their professional vantage point enabled them to reach value-free conclusions. The 'new' European sociologists of that era were mostly positivists (still a term of approval), believed that they were following the methods of the natural sciences, and their aims were to describe accurately, to identify causes and consequences, and not to pass value judgements. The work of America's Chicago School (see pp. 20–21) was a model to which they could refer. This is how European sociology entered what can be recalled as a golden age in terms of its ability to address wider audiences. Sociologists reported on patterns of family and community life in 'slum' neighbourhoods. In Britain, Michael Young and Peter Willmott's book, *Family and Kinship in East London* (1957), received extensive press coverage. Middle-class England learnt, in many cases for the first time, that Eastenders and their counterparts in other cities were not depraved and suffering but enjoyed warm and supportive kin and neighbourly relationships that made other classes envious.

This was the era when Western countries were developing welfare states (see pp. 30–31). Sociologists were mostly supporters of this political project. They set about measuring the ways and the extent to which people's lives were being improved: changes in risks of poverty, and in working-class children's educational opportunities, for example. At that time sociology had the ear of governments. Sociology was offering a new kind of scientific evidence. The research usually concluded that the post-war reforms had not made enough difference, or that the reforms were having unintended and unwelcome consequences such as the destruction of supportive inner-city neighbourhood communities. However, investigators were able to recommend policy changes. If relative poverty was a new problem, a solution could be to peg welfare benefits to earnings rather than an absolute subsistence level. If rehousing to suburban council estates was destroying communities, maybe the new settlements could be designed to foster interaction among neighbours. If juvenile delinquency was subcultural, a likely answer was detached youth work. If working-class children remained under-represented in academic secondary schools, a plausible solution could be to educate all secondary age children in comprehensives. If working-class children were disadvantaged by starting school without the language skills of the typical middle-class child, an answer could be language enrichment during the early years. If middle-class parents were the more likely to visit their children's schools and support their children's progress, why not take schools into working-class neighbourhoods with home visits and displays of children's work in local shops? This advice was heeded. Sociology was influential, for a short while. Its influence was based on its manifest, factual, value-free character, carefully separating hard evidence from researchers' opinions. Also, sociology was still in the pre-computer age. The statistics were simple and the prose was straightforward – comprehensible to civil servants, newspaper journalists and students who flocked to the subject and made sociology a standard campus discipline throughout the Western world.

What went wrong? Just about everything. The reforms proposed by sociologists did not deliver. Social class inequalities in educational attainments remained as wide as ever. Planned communities failed to materialise. Rates of juvenile delinquency continued to rise. Policymakers lost confidence in sociology. Sociologists lost confidence in the possibility of reforming capitalism and many decided that the entire system needed to be replaced. Marxism swept into sociology. Positivism was attacked. 'Softer' kinds of research incorporating symbolic interactionist ideas were favoured. Policymakers have remained more impressed by the harder evidence offered by other social sciences such as economics. Its respect for Marxism set sociology outside the limits of mainstream political debate. Western economies began the transformation into post-industrialism. Neo-liberalism became the new orthodoxy in economic policy and in the process the societies began to become post-welfare. Reform ceased to mean spending more on welfare. The new trends were towards tighter targetting and seeking better value per unit of spending.

Here the criticism of mainstream post-war sociological research that concerns us is the attack on its claimed value-freedom. Critics argued that investigators may have set aside their own values, only to serve the ends of more powerful groups. In the words of American social scientist Loren Baritz (1928–2009), they had become 'servants of power' (Baritz, 1974). Baritz himself drew examples mainly from the uses of social science in industry where research was being used to assist managers to improve workforce morale, reduce absences and increase productivity. Sociologists' research was more likely to be used by government departments and agencies to assist in fine-tuning income maintenance and education policies, crime prevention and the treatment of offenders, and urban planning. Alvin Gouldner (1920–1980), an eminent American sociologist of that era, argued that the compromises required would create a crisis in sociology itself (Gouldner, 1971). He drew attention to the contradiction between mainstream sociology's claims to value-freedom, the searing critiques of welfare capitalism that the discipline was producing, and the manner in which the research labour of sociologists was being used.

There has been a subsequent split rather than a life-and-death crisis in sociology. Some regard the value of their research to governments and businesses as a compliment rather than a criticism. They argue that this is the only way in which they can hope to make a difference. In any case, academic sociologists have come under increasing pressure to secure external research funding. This may be from state-funded research councils whose remit includes supporting 'basic' research (without foreseen applications) but these councils are under increasing pressure to demonstrate 'impact'. In any case, much of the funding for social research flows directly from government departments who want policies and programmes evaluated, and who want social trends to be monitored. Sociologists who work in this research industry are now typically part of interdisciplinary, multidisciplinary or transdisciplinary teams. In practice the difference is blurred, but the key distinction is always between where separate subject specialists make their specialist contributions which are then integrated, and where different specialists' skills and perspectives are blended into new emergent disciplines – education studies, family studies, urban studies and so on.

Sociology which offers its techniques, technical expertise, bereft of any value judgements, is professional in a twenty-first-century sense. The professional is not a moral guide or guardian. Whether they are sociologists, lawyers, accountants or engineers, professional skills and advice are made available to whoever is prepared to pay, or maybe (in the case of sociologists) whoever will just listen and implement. The French sociologist Jean-François Lyotard (1924–1998) has argued that a feature of our post-modern condition is that knowledge is judged on 'performativity', that is, use value, and that we have thereby waylaid the 'grand narratives' which, true or false, once gave meaning to people's lives and told us where the world was heading. This, according to Lyotard (1984), is the empty triumph of rationalism.

Sociology today has a split personality. It is partly within, and partly outside and critical of any assimilation into wider power structures. Clients and users of research are sometimes non-governmental organisations, but they are unlikely to be able to fund research or do much implementing unless they are really *quangos* (quasi-autonomous nongovernmental organisations), largely funded by the state and therefore required to implement state policies.

CRITICAL SOCIOLOGIES

All sociologists can claim to be critical in the term's everyday meaning. Those who evaluate government programmes (to improve 'failing' schools, or to restart the long-term unemployed, for example) do not necessarily endorse the programmes themselves or the thinking on which they are based. Evaluation studies often demonstrate that government measures are not working as planned. If the investigators are not allowed to tell it straight in the official published reports of the research, they can do so in books, conference papers and journal articles. In any case, government departments want researchers to interrogate their policies as strenuously as possible. They do not want to be assured that all is well up until the point when failure becomes obvious to all. 'Critical' in the sense of being sceptical, questioning, is an adjective to which all sociologists have an equal claim.

However, 'critical' was a given a narrower meaning by the Frankfurt School. Chicago and Frankfurt are sociology's only examples of places which have become 'schools' through developing distinctive bodies of theory and method. From the 1890s until the Second World War, Chicago was developing a distinctive brand of theoretically informed but simultaneously research-based sociology, employing a combination of quantitative and qualitative methods. Frankfurt was in Europe, geographically and (in the 1920s) intellectually. Frankfurt School is the name given to the work undertaken at the Institute of Social Research which opened in Frankfurt in 1923. Its leading researchers were Marxists and Jews, and they and their institute relocated to New York after Hitler took control in Germany in 1933. The institute, and some of its original members, returned to Frankfurt in 1949. The institute formally closed in 1969 but its intellectual legacy remains alive, principally today in the work of the German sociologist Jürgen Habermas (b. 1929).

The principal original members of the Frankfurt School included Theodor Adorno, Walter Benjamin, Erich Fromm, Max Horkheimer and Herbert Marcuse. They felt that Marxism needed to be developed to address the changes that had taken place since Marx's lifetime, and particularly to address the post-First World War situation. The theory needed to be able to explain why so many members of Europe's working classes were joining Fascist rather than socialist movements (see Chapter 3, pp. 26–7). The Frankfurt researchers also felt that they needed to appraise critically the society that the Bolsheviks were creating in the Soviet Union. Had the Bolshevik take-over really been a proletariat-led revolution? Was the Soviet Union becoming a genuine workers' state given the unfavourable circumstances? The proletariat had been expected to seize power initially in the most advanced capitalist countries, not in still semi-feudal Russia. Members of the Frankfurt School wrote about the 'culture industry'. After migrating to the USA they found the dominant popular culture just as oppressive, albeit in a different way, as Fascism in Germany. By then some members of the Frankfurt School were pioneering the assimilation into Marxism of Freudian ideas. However, what most concerns us here is the sense in which the school was trying to create a distinctively critical type of sociology.

The Frankfurt School treated sociology, as it had developed in Europe up until the First World War, as part of an 'Enlightenment Project' which had been launched during the Age of Reason in the seventeenth and eighteenth centuries. The hope of the Enlightenment was that through reason people would understand and gain control over their environments (natural, social and political), and thereby experience emancipation. Hegel and Comte shared this vision. However, the Frankfurt School realised (or claimed) that up until their present time, modern reasoning had become another set of controls over most people's lives. Rather than being liberated by reason and the resulting developments in science and technology, people's lives were being subjected to forever more rigorous and detailed control. This applied to people's lives at work. In addition, governments had been empowered in subjugating their citizens, and had thereby been able to lead their countries into the disastrous First World War. The

Frankfurt School's critical sociology had, first of all, to be self-critical, querying its own assumptions. The big idea was that a truly emancipatory theory would need to reject instrumental reasoning, the ends-means thinking that Weber had identified as the hallmark of the modern world. This use of reason enabled people to be treated as means. In so far as sociology, and Marxism, incorporated this kind of reasoning, the Frankfurt School claimed that these modes of thought were more likely to become instruments of oppression than emancipation (see Connerton, 1976; Held, 1980).

Later in the twentieth century the French philosopher Michel Foucault (see Chapter 6, pp. 104–5) echoed these ideas. Towards the end of the twentieth century the French sociologist, Jean-François Lyotard (1924–1998), updated the arguments. Lyotard attached considerable importance to the computer, but he was writing well before the Internet era. As noted above, Lyotard's main claim was that 'performativity' had become the key test of the value of all knowledge. Performativity refers to use value: knowledge as a productive force that can be bought and sold. An effect, according to Lyotard, has been to fragment knowledge, depriving people of an ability to understand their societies' places in history and their own positions within their societies. All such ideas (which Lyotard called 'grand narratives') are sidelined as the business of experts (Lyotard, 1984).

One view of 'the post-modern condition' is that the Enlightenment Project has now run its course, manifestly failed, must be abandoned, and that emancipation requires us to recognise that there are no objectively right answers but numerous possible ways of reading any text or viewing society. According to this view, we should embrace our liberation to see things in different ways. The fragmentation of sociology into a series of standpoints (feminist, post-colonial, queer and so on) liberates all those who are part of these tendencies to see the world in their own ways.

Jürgen Habermas (1976, 1984) dissents, claiming that the Enlightenment Project has not failed, but is simply incomplete. He contends that the basic, most elementary and essential form of social life arises through free and open dialogue, what he calls an 'ideal speech situation' which creates a 'public sphere'. Under these conditions people employ 'communicative reason' which is engaged in for its own sake, and leads to 'communicative action' in which people are interested in each other for their own sakes. The clearest examples are in families (into which, according to Habermas, the public sphere tends to have collapsed in modern societies), but a public sphere can extend much wider. Through free and open dialogue people are said to create intersubjective 'lifeworlds'. According to Habermas, these lifeworlds are the sole source of knowledge that can be agreed to be correct, both factually and morally. From the basis of these lifeworlds people are said to create institutions (political parties, businesses and so on) in which action is governed by 'instrumental reason'. Here people are treated as means, as commodities, not for their own sakes but to enable one party to achieve its ends. Institutions owe their legitimacy to their grounding in lifeworlds. This enables people to feel that institutions belong to and are acting for them. However, Habermas argues that institutions, ruled by instrumental reason, are not only able to decouple themselves from lifeworlds and communicative reason, but may actually colonise these lifeworlds, a condition said to characterise present-day societies. The outcomes are said to be individuals who feel anxious and that their lives are meaningless, and a 'legitimation crisis' in the entire systems. The solution, according to Habermas, is reborn public spheres, not just in families but in new social movements in which free and open dialogue is maintained.

These are abstract ideas, but they can metamorphose into a distinctive down-to-earth type of public sociology, perhaps best exemplified in the intentions (but not yet in the achievements) of Michael Burawoy. He was educated in Britain, qualified in mathematics at Cambridge University in 1968, went to work as a personnel officer in a Zambia copper mine operated by the Anglo-American Corporation, took an MA and moved towards sociology while in Zambia, and has been USA-based from the 1970s onwards. While gathering material for his Ph.D. in Chicago he was employed as a machine operator in an engineering workshop. Towards the end of the 1980s he was employed at a steel works in Communist Hungary. Burawoy describes such periods of employment as summer vacation jobs. In the early-1990s he was employed in a furniture plant in an Arctic region of post-Soviet Russia. Burawoy admits that he has always been regarded as an incompetent worker by shop-floor colleagues, but his methods and output have won applause in sociology. Burawoy (2005) advocates a particular kind of public sociology. This is different from professional sociology where the audience comprises other sociologists. It is also different from policy sociology, sometimes conducted for but always intended to influence the policies and practices of government departments or other organisations. Ideal typically, Burawoy's public sociology is practised in a Habermasian public sphere. Ethnography through participant observation is the core research method. There is free and open dialogue with the subjects, who ideal typically become partners in both the production and implementation of sociological knowledge.

Feminism and anti-racism in the West can be cited as successful examples of new social movements within which this kind of public sociology has been conducted. Future successes may include environmental and peace movements. The working class is still the big challenge for Michael Burawoy, and for sociology more broadly.

Today there are many sociologies, and individuals can move between them during their careers. Indeed, it is possible to wear several sociological 'hats' within a single career stage. Professional sociology (where other sociologists make-up the core audience) still produces its occasional public intellectual who addresses the wider public via the media. There is plenty of policy sociology. Practising Michael Burawoy's public sociology is a tougher challenge. A more comfortable kind of critical sociology is more commonplace. It simply criticises all other types of sociology. Unless researchers have subjects who are also partners, in truth these critical sociologists are practising an alternative form of professional sociology.

SOCIOLOGY TODAY

There is no danger that sociology will decompose. We can disagree on our preferred roles and play different roles in the wider society. We can use different research methods and remain in dispute about the most basic elements of social life. We stay bound by common interests in large-scale historical transformations and social divisions. These topics create the distinctive niche for sociology that Durkheim sought. Social change makes it impossible for sociology to stagnate. It has always been and remains an inherently lively subject. There is always something new and important to investigate.

Transformations unfold over decades, sometimes centuries, rather than just years. At present successive modern transformations are all in process, fading in some countries and just commencing in others. The original Enlightenment Project, the battle for reason, is ongoing. Industrialisation, urbanisation and demands for democracy are only now in their early stages in many parts of the world. In these countries the take-off is occurring in twenty-first-century global conditions. Countries and some individuals' lives are leaping directly from traditional villages into the digital age. This same transformation, albeit at a more advanced stage, is still in process in countries where it began over two centuries ago. George Ritzer (1993) has argued that rationalisation (which Max Weber regarded as the master trend in the modernisation of life) is only now spreading from manufacturing into consumer services, with an outcome that Ritzer terms 'McDonaldization'.

Building social democracy began when the political franchise began to be extended to all classes of people, and when modern state welfare provisions were first introduced, initially in nineteenth-century Germany when Otto von Bismarck (1815–1898) was the first Chancellor of the unified country from 1871 until 1890. He introduced state insurance schemes covering health, accidents, disability and old age between 1883 and 1889. In the UK, old age state pensions date from 1909 and national insurance (covering unemployment and sickness) from 1911. Social democracy is still marching onwards, but in different ways in different places. The older social democracies are still extending full citizen rights to women, ethnic and religious minorities, people with different sexual orientations, and with different abilities and disabilities, though in these same countries the most powerful current trends are rolling-back state welfare. Simultaneously, new EU member states are being drawn into 'social Europe'; while in other parts of the world the drive is still to extend basic health care and education to everyone.

However, the most powerful currents of change in all parts of the present-day world are those that have transformed European and North American countries into post-industrial societies. This has involved massive shifts of employment between business sectors (from extractive and manufacturing industries into services) and between occupational classes (smaller working classes and enlarged middle classes). These shifts have coincided with the financialisation and globalisation of capitalism, and the spread of digital technologies. Most national governments, urged by transnational economic regulators (the World Bank, the International Monetary Fund, the World Trade Organisation, the European Union) have responded by adopting neo-liberal policies which involve deregulating all markets, curbing government spending, hence trimming parts of their welfare states, thereby enabling the countries to adopt investor friendly tax regimes (reducing and making taxes on incomes and profits less progressive).

This latest transformation is still in full flow and is raising a series of unresolved issues. At present neo-liberalism is manifestly failing to deliver on all its promises. People were told that opening up global markets would be a win-win measure: that there would be no casualties. In the event, there have been some (at least short-term) losers. Workers in Western Europe and North America have faced job competition from labour in lower cost countries. Jobs either go offshore or migrants compete for those that remain 'at home'. It was once claimed that less skilled 'body work' would be exported from first world countries whose own labour forces would earn much higher salaries doing high-skilled, high value-added knowledge work. This is not how things have worked out. There have been steep increases in the supply of highly educated labour in all world regions. Digitalisation makes it easy to export not just routine information processing but also research, design and product development.

Young people in Europe and North America have been told that they should regard their education as a private investment in their own human capital which will be repaid with interest when they obtain commensurate employment. These promises are being broken. In the USA the average starting salary offered to college degree holders declined in real terms between 1973 and 2005. In the UK a third of the higher education graduates who took out government loans from 1998 onwards had still made no repayments in 2010 because their pay had remained beneath the threshold that triggered payback (Brown et al., 2011, pp. 116, 118).

Economic growth in Asia, Africa and Latin America is boosting global demand for commodities, which is likely to lead to progressively rising prices for energy, other minerals and food. Growth rates in Western Europe and North America since the 1970s have been lower than during the 30 years from 1945 to 1975. The more modest gains from growth are now being swallowed by addressing the costs of growth – pollution and the threat of ecological disaster, possibly catastrophic climate change.

The eventual outcomes of the latest transformation are likely to be decades ahead. They are still uncertain. Sociology is the sole discipline that explores all the associations between the economic, political, social and cultural dimensions of these changes. It alone seeks to distinguish the drivers and beneficiaries from victims and losers. The issues are huge and challenging. New sociological minds are needed because the existing books and journals contain no answers.

Bibliography

Abel-Smith, B. and Townsend, P. (1966), *The Poor and the Poorest*, London: Bell.

Adorno, T., Frenkel-Brunswick, E., Levinson, D. and Sanford, R. (1950 [1991]), *The Authoritarian Personality*, New York: Norton.

Andreski, S. (ed.) (1974), *The Essential Comte*, London: Croom Helm.

Arnett, J.J. (2005), *Emerging Adulthood: The Winding Road from Late Teens Through the Twenties*, Oxford: Oxford University Press.

Banton, M. (1997), *Ethnic and Racial Consciousness*, 2nd edn, Harlow: Longman.

Baritz, L. (1974), *The Servants of Power: A History of the Use of Social Science in American Industry*, Westport: Greenwood.

Baudrillard, J. (1998), *The Consumer Society*, London: Sage.

Bauman, Z. (1998), *Work, Consumerism and the New Poor*, Buckingham: Open University Press.

Bauman, Z. (2006), *Liquid Times: Living in an Age of Uncertainty*, Cambridge: Polity.

Beauvoir, S. de (1972 [1997]), *The Second Sex*, London: Vintage.

Beck, U. (1992), *Risk Society: Towards a New Modernity*, London: Sage.

Beck, U. and Beck-Gernsheim, E. (1995), *The Normal Chaos of Love*, Cambridge: Polity Press.

Beck, U. and Beck-Gernsheim, E. (2009), 'Global generations and the trap of methodological nationalism for a cosmopolitan turn in the sociology of youth and generation', *European Sociological Review*, 25, 25–36.

Becker, H.S. (1963), *Outsiders: Studies in the Sociology of Deviance*, Glencoe: Free Press.

Bell, D. (1960), *The End of Ideology*, New York: Collins.

Bell, D. (1974), *The Coming of Post-Industrial Society*, New York: Basic Books.

Bhasker, R. (1975 [1997]), *A Realist Theory of Science*, London: Verso.

Bourdieu, P. (1984), *Distinction: A Social Critique of the Judgement of Taste*, London: Routledge.

Bourdieu, P. and Passeron, J.D. (1977), *Reproduction in Education, Culture and Society*, London: Sage.

Brown, P., Lauder, H. and Ashton, D. (2011), *The Global Auction*, Oxford: Oxford University Press.

Bulmer, M. (1984), *The Chicago School of Sociology*, Chicago: University of Chicago Press.

Burawoy, M. (2005), 'For public sociology', *American Sociological Review*, 70, 4–28.

Burnham, J. (1943), *The Managerial Revolution*, London: Putman.

Castells, M. (1996), *The Rise of the Network Society*, Oxford: Blackwell.

Castles, S. (1973), *Immigrant Workers and the Class Structure in Western Europe*, London: Oxford University Press.

Castles, S. and Miller, M.J. (2003), *The Age of Migration*, Basingstoke: Palgrave Macmillan.

Centre for Economic Performance (2010), *Immigration and the UK Labour Market: The Evidence from Economic Research*, Centre for Economic Performance, London School of Economics, London.

Chomsky, N. (1957), *Syntactic Structures*, The Hague: Mouton.

Connerton, B. (ed.) (1976), *Critical Sociology*, Harmondsworth: Penguin.

Crosland, A. (1956), *The Future of Socialism*, London: Cape.

Davis, K. and Moore, W.E. (1945), 'Some principles of stratification', *American Sociological Review*, 10, 242–9.

Dawe, A. (1971), 'The two sociologies', in Thompson, K. and Tunstall, J. (eds), *Sociological Perspectives*, Harmondsworth: Penguin.

Dilthey, W. (Rickman, H.P. ed.) (1976), *W. Dilthey, Selected Writings*, Cambridge: Cambridge University Press.

Durkheim, É. (1893 [1938]), *The Division of Labour in Society*, Glencoe: Free Press.

Durkheim, É. (1895 [1938]), *The Rules of Sociological Method*, Glencoe: Free Press

Durkheim, É. (1897 [1970]), *Suicide: A Study in Sociology*, London: Routledge.

Durkheim, É. (1912 [1956]), *The Elementary Forms of Religious Life*, London: Allen and Unwin.

Edwards, R. and Weller, S. (2010), 'Trajectories of youth to adulthood: choice and structure for young people before and during the recession', *21st Century Society*, 5, 125–36.

Esping-Anderson, G. (1990), *The Three Worlds of Welfare Capitalism*, New Jersey: Princeton University Press.

Evans, K. and Heinz, W.R. (1994), *Becoming Adults in England and Germany*, London: Anglo-German Foundation.

Fanon, F. (1967 [1990]), *The Wretched of the Earth*, Harmondsworth: Penguin.

Foucault, M. (1963 [1973]), *The Birth of the Clinic*, London: Tavistock.

Foucault, M. (1975 [1977]), *Discipline and Punish: The Birth of the Prison*, London: Tavistock.

Foucault, M. (1976 [1980]), *The History of Sexuality*, New York: Random House.

Frank, A.G. (1969), *Capitalism and Underdevelopment in Latin America*, New York: Monthly Review Press.

Freud, S. (1927), *The Future of an Illusion*, London: Hogarth Press.

Freud, S. (1930), *Civilization and its Discontents*, London: Hogarth Press.

Friedman, M. (1981), *Studies in the Quantity and Theory of Money*, Chicago: University of Chicago Press.

Fukuyama, F. (1992), *The End of History and the Last Man*, London: Penguin.

Galbraith, J.K. (1967), *The New Industrial State*, Harmondsworth: Penguin.

Garfinkel, H. (1967), *Studies in Ethnomethodology*, Engelwood Cliffs: Prentice Hall.

Gerth, H.H. and Mills, C.W. (eds) (1946), *From Max Weber: Essays in Sociology*, New York: Oxford University Press.

Giddens, A. (1979), *Central Problems in Social Theory*, London: Macmillan.

Giddens, A. (1984), *The Constitution of Society*, Cambridge: Polity Press.

Giddens, A. (1991), *Modernity and Self-Identity: Self and Society in the Late Modern Age*, California: Stanford University Press.

Giddens, A. (1992), *The Transformation of Intimacy: Sexuality, Love, and Eroticism in Modern Societies*, California: Stanford University Press.

Giddens, A. (1998), *The Third Way: The Renewal of Social Democracy*, Cambridge: Polity Press.

Ginsberg, M. (1947), *Essays in Sociology and Social Philosophy*, London: Heinemann.

Glaser, B. and Strauss, A. (1968), *The Discovery of Grounded Theory*, London: Weidenfeld and Nicolson.

Gluckman, M. (ed.) (1964), *Closed Systems and Open Minds*, London: Oliver and Boyd.

Goffman, E. (1959), *The Presentation of Self in Everyday Life*, New York: Doubleday Anchor.

Goffman, E. (1961), *Asylums*, Harmondsworth: Penguin.

Goffman, E. (1964), *Stigma: Notes on the Management of Identity*, Harmondsworth: Penguin.

Goffman, E. (1974), *Frame Analysis*, Harmondsworth: Penguin.

Goldthorpe, J.H., Llewellyn, C. and Payne, C. (1980 [1987]), *Social Mobility and Class Structure in Britain*, Oxford: Clarendon Press.

Goldthorpe, J.H., Lockwood, D., Bechhofer, F. and Platt, J. (1969), *The Affluent Worker in the Class Structure*, London: Cambridge University Press.

Gouldner, A.W. (1971), *The Coming Crisis of Western Sociology*, London: Heinemann.

Habermas, J. (1976), *Legitimation Crisis*, London: Heinemann.

Habermas, J. (1984, 1988), *The Theory of Communicative Action*, 2 Vols, Cambridge: Polity.

Hakim, C. (2004), *Key Issues in Women's Work: Female Diversity and the Polarisation of Women's Employment*, London: Glasshouse.

Hall, S. and Jacques, M. (eds) (1983), *The Politics of Thatcherism*, London: Lawrence and Wishart.

Halsey, A.H., Heath, A.F. and Ridge, J.M. (1980), *Origins and Destinations*, Oxford: Clarendon Press.

Held, D. (1980), *Introduction to Critical Theory*, London: Hutchinson.

Henderson, S., Holland, J., McGrellis, S., Sharpe, S. and Thomson, R. (2007), *Inventing Adulthoods: A Biographical Approach to Youth Transitions*, London: Sage.

Hobhouse, L.T. (1915), *Morals in Evolution: A Study of Comparative Ethics*, London: Chapman and Hall.

Huntington, S.P. (1996), *The Clash of Civilizations and the Remaking of World Order*, New York: Simon and Schuster.

Husserl, E. (1970), *The Crisis of the European Sciences and Transcendental Phenomenology*, Evanston: Northwestern University Press.

Inglehart, R. (1977), *The Silent Revolution*, New Jersey: Princeton University Press.

Inglehart, R. (1997), *Modernization and Postmodernization*, New Jersey: Princeton University Press.

Jackson, B. and Marsden, D. (1962), *Education and the Working Class*, London: Routledge.

Kerr, C., Dunlop, J.T., Harbison, F.H. and Myers, C.A. (1960), *Industrialism and Industrial Man: The Problems of Labour and Management in Economic Growth*, Cambridge, MA: Harvard University Press.

Kuhn, T. (1962), *The Structure of Scientific Revolutions*, Chicago: Chicago University Press.

Lash, S. and Urry, J. (1987), *The End of Organised Capitalism*, Oxford: Polity Press.

Lemert, E.M. (1967), *Human Deviance, Social Problems and Social Control*, New Jersey: Prentice Hall.

Lévi-Strauss, C. (1969), *Totemism*, Harmondsworth: Penguin.

Lévi-Strauss, C. (1972), *The Savage Mind*, London: Weidenfeld and Nicolson.

Lynd, R.S. and Lynd, H.M. (1929), *Middletown: A Study in Contemporary American Culture*, New York: Harcourt, Brace and Co.

Lynd, R.S. and Lynd, H.M. (1937), *Middletown in Transition: A Study in Cultural Conflicts*, New York: Harcourt, Brace and Co.

Lyotard, J.-F. (1984), *The Postmodern Condition: A Report on Knowledge*, Manchester: Manchester University Press.

Mannheim, K. (1929 [1936]), *Ideology and Utopia*, London: Routledge.

Marcuse, H. (1955 [1991]), *Eros and Civilization: A Philosophical Inquiry into Freud*, Boston: Beacon Press.

Marcuse, H. (1964), *One Dimensional Man: Studies in the Ideology of Advanced Industrial Society*, London: Routledge.

Marshall, T.H. (1963), *Sociology at the Crossroads*, London: Heinemann.

Marx, K. (1970), *Capital*, London: Lawrence and Wishart.

Marx, K. and Engels, F. (1848 [1985]), *The Communist Manifesto*, London: Penguin.

McClellan, D. (1975), *Marx*, London: Fontana/Collins.

Mead, G.H. (1934), *Mind, Self and Society*, Chicago: Chicago University Press.

Merton, R.K. (1949), *Social Theory and Social Structure*, Glencoe: Free Press.

Miles, S. (1998), *Consumerism – As a Way of Life*, London: Sage.

Miliband, R. (1969), *The State in Capitalist Society*, London: Weidenfeld and Nicolson.

Miliband, R. (1973), *Parliamentary Socialism*, London: Merlin Press.

Mills, C.W. (1959), *The Sociological Imagination*, New York: Oxford University Press.

Pareto, V. (1973), *The Mind and Society: A Treatise on General Sociology*, New York: Dover.

Parsons, T. (1937), *The Structure of Social Action*, New York: Free Press.

Parsons, T. (1951), *The Social System*, London: Routledge.

Parsons, T. (1966), *Societies: Evolutionary and Comparative Perspectives*, Engelwood Cliffs: Prentice-Hall.

Patterson, S. (1963), *Dark Strangers*, London: Tavistock.

Popper, K.R. (1945), *The Open Society and its Enemies*, London: Routledge.

Popper, K.R. (1957), *The Poverty of Historicism*, London: Routledge.

Popper, K.R. (1963), *Conjectures and Refutations: The Growth of Scientific Knowledge*, London: Routledge.

Reiss, E. (1996), *Marx: A Clear Guide*, London: Pluto Press.

Rex, J. (1970), *Race Relations in Sociological Theory*, London: Weidenfeld and Nicolson.

Riesman, D. (1952), *The Lonely Crowd: A Study of the Changing American Character*, New Haven: Yale University Press.

Ritzer, G. (1993), *The McDonaldization of Society*, Thousand Oaks: Pine Forge Press.

Said, E.W. (1978 [1995]), *Orientalism*, Harmondsworth: Penguin.

Savage, M. (2010), *Identities and Social Change in Britain since 1940: The Politics of Method*, Oxford: Oxford University Press.

Savage, M., Bagnall, G. and Longhurst, B. (2005), *Globalization and Belonging*, London: Sage.

Schutz, A. (1972), *The Phenomenology of the Social World*, London: Heinemann.

Segal, L. (2007), *Slow Motion: Changing Masculinities, Changing Men*, Basingstoke: Palgrave Macmillan.

Simmel, G. (1903 [1950]), 'The metropolis and mental life', in Wolff, K. (ed.), *The Sociology of Georg Simmel*, New York: Free Press.

Singer, P. (1983), *Hegel*, Oxford: Oxford University Press.

Smith, A.D. (1986), *The Ethnic Origins of Nations*, Oxford: Blackwell.

Smith, D.E. (1990), *The Conceptual Practices of Power: A Feminist Sociology of Knowledge*, Boston: Northeastern University Press.

Thomas, W.I. (1927), 'The behavior pattern and the situation', *Publications of the American Sociological Society: Papers and Proceeding*, 22nd Annual Meeting, Vol. 22, 1–13.

Thompson, K. (1976), *Auguste Comte: The Foundations of Sociology*, London: Nelson.

Tönnies, F. (1887 [1955]), *Community and Association*, London: Routledge.

Walker, C.R. and Guest, R.H. (1952), *The Man on the Assembly Line*, Cambridge, MA: Harvard University Press.

Warner, W.L. (1948), *The Social System of a Modern Factory*, New Haven: Yale University Press.

Warner, W.L. (1949), *The Social Systems of American Ethnic Groups*, New Haven: Yale University Press.

Warner, W.L. (1950), *The Status System of a Modern Community*, New Haven: Yale University Press.

Warner, W.L. (1959), *The Living and the Dead: A Study of the Symbolic Life of Americans*, New Haven: Yale University Press.

Warner, W.L. and Lunt, P. (1941), *The Social Life of a Modern Community*, New Haven: Yale University Press.

Weber, M. (1905 [1930]), *The Protestant Ethic and the Spirit of Capitalism*, London: Allen and Unwin.

Welzel, C., Inglehart, R. and Kingemann, H.-D. (2003), 'The theory of human development: a cross-cultural analysis', *European Journal of Political Research*, 42, 341–79.

Winch, P. (1958 [1990]), *The Idea of a Social Science and its Relation to Philosophy*, London: Routledge.

Wright, E.O. (2000), *Class Counts: Student Edition*, New York: Cambridge University Press.

Wrong, D.H. (1961), 'The oversocialized conception of man in modern sociology', *American Sociological Review*, 26, 183–93.

Young, M. and Willmott, P. (1957), *Family and Kinship in East London*, London: Routledge.

Index

reliability 124, 126
religion 15, 18, 22–3, 24, 92
Renaissance 109
research ethics *see* ethics
research methods 108–36
response rates 122
revolutions 7
Rex, J. 77, 158
Rice, C. 72
Rickman, H.P. 154
Ridge, J.M. 156
Riesman, D. 19, 158
risk society 43
Ritzer, G. 25, 150, 158
Rousseau, J.-J. 15
Rowntree, S. 27, 118

Said, E.W. 82, 158
salariat 53
sampling 118, 119–21, 129–30
Sanford, R. 153
Savage, M. 76, 132, 140, 158
Schutz, A. 97, 99, 158
science 2, 3, 23, 96, 109–16, 143
scientific management 39
Segal, L. 67, 158
self 98, 100, 105
self-employment *see* petit bourgeoisie
service class 53
sexual orientations 4, 48, 84–5
Sharpe, S. 156
significant other 98
signs *see* symbols
Simmel, G. 19, 22, 158
Singer, P. 11, 158
slavery 20, 76, 77, 78
Smith, A. 9, 139–40
Smith, A.D. 77, 158
Smith, D.E. 71, 158
snowball sampling 130
social anthropology 15, 47, 126, 134
social class 4, 12, 34–5, 42, 46–64
social democracy 4, 29–36, 38, 50, 67, 150–151
social divisions 4–5, 46–86
social facts 89–91, 100–101, 107
social market economy 4, 29–30
social mobility 35
social structure 88, 89–96
social system 88, 89–96

socialisation 94–5
Soros, G. 111
Spencer, H. 10
SPSS 118
standpoint sociology 71, 148
statistical methods 118–19
status 52
stigma 100
Strauss, A. 155
structural functionalism *see* functionalism
structuralism 103–4
structuration 105–6
student movements 32–3
subaltern sociology 82
suicide 17, 89–90, 100
surplus value 12–13, 49, 69
surveys 119–23
symbolic interaction 99–102, 113, 135, 144
symbols 98, 99

Taylor, F.W. 39
Taylorism 39
texts, analysis of 123–4
Thatcher, M. 37, 72, 88
third way 44–5
Thomas, W.I. 99–100, 158
Thompson, K. 9, 158
Thomson, R. 156
time use studies 131
Tönnies, F. 10, 19, 22, 25, 158
total institutions 100
Townsend, P. 34, 153
trade unions 37, 38, 42, 52, 61
traditional action 24–5
transformations 3, 5, 7–45
triangulation 114–15, 119

underclass 41, 53
under-development 78
Understanding Society 44, 131
United Nations 47, 74, 131, 141
unobtrusive research 123–4, 134
urbanisation 3, 20–21
Urry, J. 38, 156
utilitarianism 9, 140

validity 124, 126
value free sociology 142–6